LADY WALKER

A STORY OF RENEWAL

BY ANNETTE FRANCIS

AnnetteFrancisAuthor@gmail.com

https://afrancisladywalker.wixsite.com/ladywalker

All poetry in this edition by Annette Francis

First KDP Printing, 2018

ISBN: 978-1-9804-2276-1

Cover design and content editing by
Michelle Hegarty of Modified Editing Services

I dedicate this book to this woman's best friend, a Welsh Collie named Jess, who picked me up when she was a puppy and I was starting over. Jess motivated me to feel the light of the sun again. She believed in me.

When standing at the base of the mountain,
body and mind are not yet geared to appreciate
the grandeur of the occasion.

— A.F.

Chapter One

I don't consider myself a climber—I'm not strong or skilled enough. Maybe if I'd discovered this soulful exertion when I was younger, I would deserve that title. Undoubtedly, I would have trained hard and competitively to program my body and mind into an accomplished mountaineer. A climber is adept at strategically taking on a mountain, geared and skilled, both physically and mentally, to tackle unforeseen challenges such as ice, snow, and winter's cold.

There's skill in judging when to use a pickaxe or ropes or knowing how to dig underground when an avalanche is hurtling near.

Instead, I'm a walker.

Walking a hill gives me a reason to abandon the duvet—I love to discover what's at the top. Hills start humble and small, portions of earth build up over time. Initially, a hill may seem stationary and unimportant, but underneath it will be alive, biding time until its growth is noticeable. Mother Nature teaches us that anything worthwhile must be nurtured and seasoned.

In the North American Ohio River Valley, native peoples known as the Hopewell designed and built mounds as early as 10 B.C., in both spiral and dome shapes which could reach nine meters tall and 305 meters wide. This has given the Hopewell tribe the nickname, "the mound builders". Archaeologists have been fascinated by and investigated the purpose of these builds. They could have been burial mounds or astronomical observatories.

When created naturally, geological activity through faulting keeps underground rocks constantly moving, causing changes that affect Earth's surface. The Himalayas in Asia, which is the tallest mountain range in the world, were once a group of small hills that continue to grow because of faulting activity.

I haven't considered a hill to be of less significance than a mountain, knowing they all show unique personalities. I've climbed steep hills that have pressured my leg and back muscles and forced me to stop for breath. In fact, some hills are more difficult to climb than mountains. Often there's only one way to the top, and I can't take hours and days walking around a giant circumference. With a hill I just go for it, straight up at a quick pace.

There are benefits to this nomadic pastime. I feel cleansed after completing a walk, regardless of whether I reached the summit. Time is forgotten unless the elements dictate the pace. Stealing tranquil moments of bliss replaced by wind and rains, often edged with lightning flashing across the sky, followed by drumming thunder. But once the time is gone from my mind, I can relax and appreciate every step. Sometimes, within an organised walking group, I've been marched to get to a certain point at a certain time. Along with my body being uncomfortable, this disturbed my natural calling. I felt cheated and under extreme pressure. This can spoil the whole experience, so now I plan my own adventures. I don't want to miss the lonesome daisy fighting to get her head above the long, tangling grass, or a rambling dog rose that has grown attached to a snapped tree.

Each walker starts off differently. You may be feeling lethargic, weak, and inadequate until you get into your stride. Alternatively, you could be one of those people who can't get there soon enough and scurry to the front. I prefer to go at a slower pace to suit my body's requirements. I have an underactive thyroid and need levothyroxine every day to regulate my metabolism, or I flake out; I know my limitations. Everyone must walk at a speed that is appropriate for them.

My walking patterns change depending on many factors: How long is the trek – a day or weeks? Is my body working on full throttle or does it lack some vital nutrients? Is my heart really in it? The truth is, some days I think I can fly to the moon and back and if I were able I would organise a North Pole trek and race with huskies in Alaska. But between these wishful moments, I'm a realist, grateful for what life has given me.

Novice walkers are easily noticed. They often allow excitement to rule and forget the consequences: burnout, fatigue, dehydration, injury, and not reaching the summit. Their heartache and disappointment can be devastating to watch.

I try to experience a relationship with every hill and mountain, a mental connection. When I first sighted mountain features and heard the voices from its unseen occupants above, my senses became charged, darting from interchanging canvases, ripped naked by the perfumes and textures of the vibrant plant life.

And, when my boots stepped off Kilimanjaro's crust, I was instantly clouded with overwhelming sadness; a sadness, I had felt before in my childhood.

When I was very young, I was roaming my village without a care in the world when a petite lady of goodness found me underneath a fairground lorry.

I was spying on the village green which was so alive with colour and delightful chaos. This happiness would graciously indulge us once a year, during the school holidays. Every good parent's pockets would be topped with coins in readiness to spoil their children.

The lady with her kind smile lifted me onto the carousel. I didn't protest. My head was already intoxicated with the melodious sounds, and my body was ready to dance. I loved the shady white horse with one eye; he was mine for a few glorious minutes. I draped my skin and bones around this large wooden form and clung for dear life, knowing I was too tiny to land safely if I fell. My white stallion took me away to a spinning magical, mystical place. I was drunk on fantasy. But the spell broke when the carousel stopped. This is what it feels like when stepping off a mountain

After a climb, walkers normally seek fellow walkers because they don't want to let the magic slip away. We are channelled while recapping every fine detail. All the way home on the bus, plane, and at the airport we still cannot let the topic go. How can you? However, eventually, we leave with our loved ones and get back into the thick of life's business, never forgetting what we left behind on the mountain.

Throughout time, holy men have emerged from mountains wiser following weeks of solitude, where they've struggled physically and mentally to digest a moment. Their conditioning and previous assumptions are trashed while digging deeper into their unconscious. Once the body and mind have been weathered, they recoat and reboot with a stronger skin and cognitive holding.

Mountain walking isn't about who can reach the summit first, but a whole body and soul experience. What is noticeable, and I have chatted with other walkers about this, is the picture I'm left holding at the end. I recognise what is important: family, quiet time to gather thoughts and, of course, the little things that cost absolutely nothing.

CHAPTER TWO

I was born in a Northern English village that meets in the middle, dividing Old Saxon and Norman rule; a tiny community called Helperby, a Viking name meaning Hialpar's Village. My family lived in a row of disjointed stone-terraced houses facing the River Swale. I was told that from the age of four my wild spirit would propel me to the back door leading to a curved path, advancing towards a half-bodied wooden gate which opened like a shutter caught in the wind. Beyond the gate was magnificent open countryside.

My dog Micky, a cross between an Alsatian and a Welsh Collie, was always in tow. We'd run freely in the warm wind before perching under my favorite willow tree, where we would watch the men fishing, reeling in the perch and barbules, until the daylight colors changed to twilight. The reflection of the sunset on the river would remind me it was time for tea. I could be left all day, my mum wouldn't worry until my stepdad walked in from work and asked, 'Where's our Bibby?' She never knew; she had my three brothers to look after, and I cannot remember her enjoying motherhood. I was a mature, introverted, undemanding child at home. Once outside I switched into a bubbly creature, dancing and singing. I was never afraid—I was well protected by Micky who wouldn't let anyone get close to me.

My lifestyle allowed me to come and go as I pleased, and the happiest times were when I was outside with Micky surrounded by fresh air and nature. Once I started school, I hated every minute of it; I felt trapped the first day when I was literally dragged into my classroom. I didn't mingle with any children apart from my brothers, who were quite tame and placid in contrast to me. I peeped through the classroom door and saw faces of the other children staring at me. It felt like they were collaborating menacingly. My tiny hand was lifted by the teacher; she pulled me inside the classroom and slammed the door. I twisted my body around to witness my mum's tilted head, smiling as if she'd had a painful tooth removed—I knew no help was there. Within seconds, I was cowering under the teacher's oak desk. Listening to the children's spiteful words and unpleasant laughter, encouraged by the impatient teacher, my impression of school was sealed.

It took the teachers and my parents nearly a year to get me to finish a full day, because as soon as I noticed the clouds rolling in the afternoon I skipped class, climbed the high stone wall, and I'd be away with the warm breeze.

My school years flew by, and life's responsibilities took over. I left the old-fashioned village and moved to Harrogate for a new job. I got married and had a family, and my outdoor life became somewhat restricted.

* * * *

Leaving school at 16, and leaving home on the same day was easy. I had just finished working six full weeks on a farm, potato picking, which gave me a wad of money. Some I hid away (I learned early how to hide things, which would be of value later) and gave the rest to my mum. Fortunately for me, the subject came up regarding what I was going to do after leaving school. The farmer and his family had taken a shine to me, and when I said I had to leave home in a matter of days they insisted I move to the farm. I was offered a full-time job working with pigs, 8 a.m. until 6 p.m., and the money was good. They provided me with a caravan, and I could pop in and out of the farmhouse to have my baths. This was the best news for me, working outside on a beautiful farm where I could roam. They even allowed me to get a puppy, Caesar, a golden Labrador who was easy to train. He was great company, and for a couple of years I was happy living in the deep country.

I saved most of my money. Strangely, every other Sunday I would thumb a lift on the roadside and walk a couple of hours until I reached the village just to check on my mum. She had become very quiet and often was pleased to see me. I would buy her little gifts—cigarettes pleased her the most! She was now chain-smoking, a habit I knew I would never take up because I remembered what it was like to be a little person growing up in foggy rooms of smokers. My mum was pretty much housebound now, and for short spells of time I felt comfortable in her company. I liked the feeling of being able to help her.

As usual, my mind was racing ahead to my future. I didn't want to get trapped in a caravan. I was a young adult in the making and wanted to finish my education. I went through several animal-related jobs: animal technology, veterinary practice, and kennels before I settled into office work. I was a touch typist and could type 60 words a minute. I worked primarily as a temp, giving me a taste of various jobs—government establishments, banks and building societies, but the best temp job I had was working for architects. Every plan and building construction was different, and my boss was happy to share his knowledge, feeding my inquisitive mind. I was popular, and employers usually offered me positions within their work force. I had a bubbly personality and was eager to learn any task asked of me. In conjunction, I attended evening college intermittently for years, collecting all manner of certification. An HND in fine art, spatial interior design, and garden design, as well as administration and secretarial qualifications (which wasn't as fun) but necessary. Later, I trained in teaching and gained a degree to lead me away from the office. I realized early that working with cubicles of people didn't suit me. I would become mentally drained by the end of the day. Owning my own space is important to me; being around negative people is contagious and detrimental to your well-being. I consider to some degree, I am an introvert.

Initially, I was at the bottom, socially-speaking. I was naive and never knew when someone cracked a joke. I didn't know what a joke was. I was considered odd by friends who didn't understand me. I hated mixing with people and it wasn't until I became a mother that I was able to let my guard down and relax. I was shocked to learn that many people lie, and don't keep their word. The importance of being honest and dutiful had been drilled into my skull from an early age. I'd been sent to high church three times a week, sporadically falling into the arms of good people, but for many years I was among unscrupulous individuals who would fabricate the truth to serve their own needs. As a result, I was a lamb among wolves until motherhood taught me to be the wolf and fight for the welfare of my cubs. And I did. I became wiser, stronger, and more comfortable around people and myself. The big world wasn't always a ball of sunshine; there were many craters of darkness to climb out of. My choice of man wasn't wise, and early, after having my babies, I was a happy solo mum. This wasn't difficult for me. I juggled work and my time around my little ones and embraced single parent status.

To this day, I still believe the best time I had in a working environment was my early days on the pig farm. One winter a farm hand had accidentally left one of the pig-pens open and, of course, the pigs escaped. But it wasn't until a few hours later that it was noted one was missing.

The whole afternoon and evening, all work on the farm came to a standstill until the pig was found. About 20 of us went wandering over many ploughed fields, walking on hard clay, looking for the runaway. A few times the pig was spotted, and the farm hands would shout and run towards her (yes, a wise female). I stationed myself at the back, watching and listening to the men, and struggled to understand how they thought they would catch her with their bare hands. Eventually, an idea came to me. It was my job to clean out the pig yards with a forklift truck after boarding the pigs into their night accommodation. I ran back to the farm in my green overalls and oversized wellies and gathered some billy band which I threw into the yellow bucket at the front of the forklift.

I jumped into the cab and drove towards the field where the four-legged fugitive was. The pig was surrounded by the men playing silly bodies, weaving in and out of each other like horses before they leaped towards the 'pig in the middle.' I had never been so amused in my life and watched with shock, their hands flying in all directions and calling the sow with words of affection. The pig outsmarted them and ran towards a gutter with hopes to cross into another field leading to a vast woodland.

Luckily, I was parked with my engine on and drove furiously towards the pig. When I had situated myself in the pig's path I exited the vehicle, waiting until I was close enough to make my move. With the pig in my sights I dropped the bucket, jamming it underneath her and, in one swift motion, raised it high, causing the pig to fall onto her back. The men, in hot pursuit of the pig, ran towards me, smothering me with compliments. By the time the farm hands had reached us I had already dismounted and lassoed the pig. As a little girl, my dad had taught me how to tie knots and make lassos; I would often practice on Micky. He was never happy about it. This amusing tale makes me smile to this day, along with the more wonderful experiences I had on the farm. The kind farm hands always treated me like a prized doll with my oversized wellington boots, baggy overalls, and my unruly hair everywhere.

* * * *

Like every baby born, I wanted to love my mum. I did at the beginning and again, at the end, just before she died. But a few things went wrong in the middle.

I can't put it all down to her being a bad parent. I rather like to think her hand was forced by fate. She told me once how she dived into marriage at 18 to get away from her uncaring uncle and auntie who had her working on their dairy farm from morning to dusk like a cart horse, along with her sister, my Auntie Jean. Jean was two years older but got out of her plight by joining a religious group when she was 17. However, she ended up spending more years chained to the church with its strict indoctrination than my mum did on the farm.

My mum took a gamble and fell in love (I think) when she married my stepdad, Jack. A good, honest man from a well-educated background, although his temper would sometimes let him down. I thought he was my enemy and encouraged Mum's mischievous whispering in my ears. She put together a case which saddened my heart when describing her frustrations and resentment of her situation. I was early in primary school and didn't understand family politics. Though I felt the heaviness she laid on me, I loved my mum and, then, her word was gold. Mum carried on feeding me lies between precious moments of openness and forthright honesty until I walked out of the house the day after I left school at age 16 when truth crashed in on me, and I realised my stepfather had been my silent support.

Looking back, I realized he had gifted me sound advice and taught me the meaning of nature's rule. He spoke cleverly about the importance of books and wrapped words around his silver tongue many times until they were tangible. History and science was his tipple, not that he ever had much time to read with work and my mum. He gave me a vintage book which weighed down my small hands, but I knew its worth even though I couldn't read at that time. His enthusiastic description brought the pages alive. His eye and hand gestures along with few selected words described to me how books take us to magical places all around the big blue marble.

I shut my eyes and ran my tiny fingers over the brown leather cover; it had that old book smell. I couldn't stop opening and closing the book, imagining wondrous adventures. I visualized the book standing arrogantly on a cold dark bookcase, waiting patiently for a curious mind to seek its wisdom. From then on, I was motivated to learn.

When I was four years old, we routinely had a fish and chip supper on Fridays. I tried to persuade my stepdad to let me walk alone, and after doing what four-year-olds do to get their own way, he shockingly gave in. I was tickled pink and jumped around like a jack in the box with my curly hair struggling to keep decorum. My chubby fingers clutched onto the oversized shopping bag and purse, nipping two printed notes, one with the queen's head and another with a list of words. Both meant nothing to me.

I waved excitedly to my stepdad and brothers smiling at me from the heavy front door before going on my first free adventure. The chip shop was only 200 yards down the lane from my house. I leaned into the five big concrete steps leading to the inside of the shop, then pulled out the purse while I joined the queue to be served. My bobbing head was everywhere, primarily looking at shoes before I tilted it higher to study the bodies taller than me, units of warm flesh boxing me in from all sides.

The situation caused me to act out of character—I kicked the man in front of me and then attacked the counter. I intended my leg to make as much noise as a four-year-old could. The man I had assaulted laughed when he peered down at me; he lifted me up and placed me on the counter. Everyone, and more importantly the lady who was serving, could see me now. The lady in a white uniform served me before the man craned my body with one long arm and placed me back on the floor. The whole shop was alive with laughter, watching my half-pint legs struggle with the shopping bag trailing behind me. I had to sit on each step and slide down until I was out of the shop, but I was feeling pleased all the way home with the fat bag.

Once home, I couldn't knock hard enough. I reverted to what worked best and kicked the oak door with all the strength I could muster. But before it opened, a familiar hand came from behind me. It was my stepfather, who was smiling and laughing at me from above. I met his gaze and smiled, too, knowing I had pleased him. He cupped my frame into his arms and carried me inside proudly before closing the door to the street.

* * * *

When my untamed hair was gathering in thickness, it caused unsought attention. My stepdad would place me on his knees and sympathetically untangle and brush the lot into a complementary fashion. It came about later, when truths poured out, that he wanted me to keep my auburn locks, while Mum had it in mind to cut it all off. And she did, just before I started school.

Years later, I asked her why she kept my hair short and was told she didn't have time to look after a girl. That about summed it up. I never had dresses, ribbons, a teddy, or a doll. For many years I would ask for a doll, as nothing else interested me. I had seen a girl at school playing with hers. It had long curly hair with a white porcelain face. I yearned to hold the doll myself and brush its hair, which was in the same fashion as mine before my mum hacked it off. Year after year I asked for the same doll and was told the same story—that they had ordered me one from the Sunday newspaper. Yet year after year I was told it got lost in the post. I stopped asking.

On reflection, I don't think my mum considered I was a girl. She never looked at me, and I stared at her discreetly when I could. I was dressed in a fashion to my brothers, with the same leather-laced shoes and plain trousers. I don't recall owning a dress until I bought one for myself out of my weekend wages. I used to run errands for the old ladies in the village when I was 11 years old and had a full weekend job as a kitchen maid to the cousin of the queen. I enjoyed being kindly bossed around by the chubby cook, an Italian lady who was vile to everyone but me. She would sit me down as if I was someone quite important (after I had done my chores, of course) and serve me with the same food given to the lady of the house, on a wooden table covered in a square embroidered white tablecloth. Patiently, I would taste the different courses of food, tiny and delicious. My 50 pence morning payment I would have gladly forfeited for this motherly attention bestowed upon me.

Baggy trousers and colourless tops were my traditional attire, but it was appropriate as the dullness helped to camouflage my being a girl. It suited my tomboy life, climbing trees and jumping across gutters. Wet, oily, and muddied up, often I'd waddle home like a drowned rat in a miserable mood, knowing Mum was going to react. On these days, after I'd had my fun living it up like Robin Hood in the woodlands, I would get a taste of her gold wedding ring when she slapped me across the face.

* * * *

I was brought up believing the man who raised me was my biological father, yet I felt uncomfortable calling him Dad, so I didn't. My stubbornness in this regard didn't smooth the running of our household, and looking back I wished I had "played the part". My instinct was proven right the day I left home when the truth was fired at me like bullets between my eyes. My mum was leaving my stepdad, and I was caught in the middle of it. I tried to convince her to stay, but she hit me hard across my left cheek with her shoe and told me that it was my fault. She didn't leave it there. She said when she was pregnant with me she bathed in hot water and drank alcohol, as well as taking medication, to abort me, but she just vomited all her insides out apart from me. She concluded I was stubborn through and through, 'just like him', then pointed to my stepdad. It was quite a revealing day; truth didn't appear on Mum's lips often. She was in full swing and needed to have a verbal clear-out! My mum then decided to go for the jugular and told me that my stepdad wasn't my dad.

My first thought was of relief. It had taken her 16 years to find these words of truth. Now I could concentrate on positive things, such as my future. But not before an overwhelming cloak of guilt draped me as I watched my stepdad, who had been sitting with his head low at the kitchen table, slide onto his knees and openly cry.

I had never seen this side of him before. He sounded like a wounded hound caught in a trap. I felt his heart drop and it didn't feel good; the air between us was deathly silent. All I could hear was my mum spouting off cruel nonsense in the fading background.

I turned to him and gave him a look of solidarity. He spoke nervously in my direction. 'You should have been mine. You have more grit and fire running through your veins than the boys put together.' His sincere words gave me strength, although I thought he had judged my brothers unfairly. I had been standing tall near the back door, for the last time. My will beckoned towards him, but I faltered. I couldn't look at his drained face portraying such disappointment and sadness.

I thought back to when my brothers and I ploughed through the fields with him, in our wellies, gathering firewood for winter. An uprooted tree crossed our path; lightning had cut through its bough. We little ones eagerly pulled and tugged at its confused branches. I slipped from the trunk which I was standing on, causing my knee to bleed. It hurt, and I felt like crying, but the gaze from my stepdad stopped me. He could be hard; he was old-school and believed it was weak to cry out loud. I didn't want to disappoint him by giving in to a little pain. I flashed a lukewarm smile, which he didn't return until I picked myself up and secured the largest log I could find and proceeded to drag it along the rugged field, greedily rushing to maintain position by his side. Only then, was I rewarded with a smile.

Now, standing at the back door, my wet eyes met his for a brief flicker, recognizing the same channel, but I abruptly broke the link and ran outside. My mind was bursting with feelings of love and compassion for a man I had believed I hated. I didn't see him again for many years.

My stepdad and I had developed an uninterrupted father/daughter relationship over later years. It came naturally with the original family unit broken up. I was living and working in Harrogate, and every other weekend I looked forward to spending Sundays with him. We'd take a stroll around the riverside and chat about wildlife, just like the old days when we used to go logging together. He always put on a colorful spread, precisely arranged on the table. He was house-proud and a stickler for the right table setting; best cutlery and matching cup and saucers from the fine china which had belonged to his gran. In the middle of the tablecloth lived the milk jug and sugar bowl. The effort he made for me made our time together quite magical in an old-fashioned way. While sipping tea and dunking ginger biscuits, he would tell me well-seasoned stories from when he was a lad, which I loved to hear. He was happy then.

He adored his grandchildren and only met Nicole twice, but commented she had the look of me, and a stubborn look to boot. We'd laugh. We had another few months of being happy before his time was up.

* * * *

I was the second child, born with a cheerful disposition and confidence. My brothers Anthony, Alan, and Jack Junior, looked up to me. They seemed grateful for me to rule the roost. They knew I had their backs when our parents argued and confused us tiny folk.

When the fights started, Anthony and Alan would sometimes scurry around the floorboards, searching for a place to hide, scampering away like little mice until the drama was over. Little Jack, however, was too young and just stayed close behind me. I would smell my brothers' nervousness. Micky, our dog, would shudder like a spider dangling from its web in case he got caught in the spectacle. He could feel the atmosphere changing from soft to prickly-cold and would pose his butt by the back door to escape the madhouse. He knew if he got caught in the middle, the stick, placed next to the hearth, would come down on his back. Many times, I saved my four-legged friend by opening the back door before joining him, often dragging Jack Junior along as well.

Not a lot of crying went on; we didn't want to be noticed. The two older boys would put their hands over their ears hoping to turn reality into a bad dream. However, blocking out the shouting and objects smashing across the room wasn't easy. Afterwards, the scene often looked like a mischievous poltergeist had been on the rampage.

Little Jack, like me, learned to ignore the noise and knew it had to run its course. I never let go of his hand; he needed me the most because he was five years younger and vulnerable. He would be glued to me and for many years followed me about like a little lamb. The bond running between us was strong. I became his bodyguard, and he loved me. His cheeky blue eyes and thick auburn hair mirrored mine, and I liked it. I loved the little chap and took total responsibility for him. I would spend hours teaching him to count and spell in the years before he went to school.

Jack Junior was never smacked. He was the youngest and their favorite, and although he looked like me my mum gave him her love and attention. She said he was their last attempt to save their marriage. I considered her last child had brought out all her goodness, and my brothers and I were pleased.

Often, I would watch the display of physical and emotional outbursts, usually caused by the "demon drink". I'd throw myself into the mix, trying to stop immature adults behaving badly. But my little body would let me down and I learned to back away.

Weekends in the kitchen was the prime spot where my parents kicked off. Generally, there was a ham simmering away in its juices, or an oversized joint of beef bordered by golden potatoes roasting in the oven. Alas, time had deformed this glorious smell and turned it into fear. The aftermath would be a silent affair, though my brothers and I would bolt down the meal irrespective of previous happenings.

Strangely, afterwards, my parents would play "happy family" with the boys and turn the day into a celebration. I was too serious and preferred to watch from a doorway, waiting for an opportunity to flee outside with Micky.

* * * *

I loved church music and would watch the organist every Sunday, wishing my tiny fingers could shadow his. I wanted him to read my mind, but he never did, and I was too shy to speak. But it wasn't long before fate intercepted and brought a nice treat for me: the opportunity to flex my fingers along the regal maple grand piano which dominated the room. I was in a little girl's heaven, which had been described to me many times at Sunday school. I was blissfully happy, too. Until my mum killed my dream and all the love I felt for her at the same time.

I had been invited up to the vicarage for tea, a privilege experienced by few. The lady of the house played for her husband and me on her piano. "The Blue Danube" by Johann Strauss, I think it was. But my memory is somewhat foggy because my eyes and ears were intent on studying how she moved across the keys in such an elegant manner.

She often gathered me up with my belongings and took me to their quiet home of blissfulness after Sunday school. After she finished playing one afternoon, the couple said they had to take their needy Jack Russell for walkabouts. They proposed I wait in the music room until their return and I happily agreed. Five or ten minutes later, I was fidgeting around in the large red leather armchair, facing the piano, knowing how it could sing, and I longed to touch its wooden skin. I didn't want to be rude and struggled hard to stay in the chair where they had left me. My head, which was awake with excitement, moved from ceiling to floor, wall to wall, staring at everything while I tried to forget the music. But my heart kept roaming back to the piano in the center of the room.

The inevitable happened, weakness took me, and a few seconds later my fingers were wiggling over the polished woodwork. The damage was done; I thought I may as well go the whole way and seated myself on the green velvet-cushioned stool. My fingers stretched for all they were worth across the ivory keys. An old hymn I used to sing in church entered my mind, called "There's a Green Hill Far Away." I sang slowly at first, a word at a time, until I could match the notes. I had quickly worked the whole song out and was speeding up the tempo and singing along.

I was so engrossed in the experience that I didn't hear the couple walk back into the room. My fingers, usually deep in the water washing dirty dishes back at home, seemed to be dancing along the keyboard. A cough disturbed me. I turned around and smiled with embarrassment when I realized I wasn't alone. My arms reached up to close the piano lid, and I gently tiptoed my feet off the stool, but accidentally slid into the welcoming arms of the lady of the house. It was a nice feeling for a nine-year-old.

After school the next day I was walking home with my brothers, and we stopped at corner of our house because we could hear piano music. We all turned our heads in different directions before mentally agreeing. Anthony said, 'That's coming from our house. Someone is playing a piano.' We ran together like a herd of deer fleeing a huntsman. I swept straight into the living room with my brothers slightly behind me.

There was our mum, playing a piano. The same one I was messing with the day before at the vicarage. It transpired that the vicar was retiring, and they were moving to a new house and wanted me to have their piano. I could hardly believe my eyes and slowly walked closer towards Mum. She didn't say a word or look around. All I heard was the sound of sorrowful music which flooded the room and my body. I was frozen on the spot. I shared her pain and joy. Recognizing her talent, I understood then she had been classically trained. Her shoulders were high, and her head and hands were positioned accurately. For the first time in my life, I had affection and pride for my mum.

Over the next two weeks, I would literally run home from school to sit with her. And while she played, she spoke to me with kindness and told me all about her life as a child, good times as well as bad. She even taught me some songs; her voice was both tuneful and soulful. I would gradually edge my chair nearer to her to feel her breath and warmth and hoped maybe she would turn and just look at me with feeling. She didn't seem to notice and concentrated on the music, happy to talk. She didn't send me away like she would have normally done. I was quite content. I felt a bond growing between us, as we both shared this passion for music. But the magic didn't last. At the end of the two-week period, the music was dead.

I have no idea to this day what happened in my mum's life to make her behave the way she did. As usual, we kids were walking home from school. Silence greeted us, and instead of rushing in through the door we snail-walked to the back door, knowing something was dreadfully wrong.

The sound of wood being chopped had replaced the sound of music. Chopping wood was one of my jobs every evening before I went to bed, to ensure we had enough kindling to start the fire in the morning. I stopped motionless, with my brothers behind me, when I spotted Mum with the axe. She was chopping through the lid of the piano; my piano, which was given to me by people who believed in me. Her face was covered in tears of pain, and a hot rage belted through her body.

I didn't think, I just screamed continually until I had nothing left to give. She didn't seem to hear or see me at all. She wouldn't stop and was too strong in mind and body to overturn her decision. I walked out of the room. It was as if someone had cut out my heart.

I spoke to my brothers, telling them to keep away from her until she calmed down, and I ran out of the house, sobbing uncontrollably. After that, I didn't try to get close to my mum again until I reached adulthood.

The piano was never mentioned again, and my mum returned to normal within a few days. I pushed the incident to the back of my mind just like she did. Soon after that, my mum and my stepfather seemed to be arguing even more, not just weekends after the pub. He was getting tired, and the older I got the less time he had for me. He was trying to keep my mum happy and would willingly jump through any hoop to do so.

I hit my 11th birthday and was starting secondary school, but it was the same time she became ill and was often in bed with pneumonia, as well as associated chest and stomach problems. She became a regular at Harrogate Hospital. The doctors could never work out what was causing her pain, even though they treated her for ulcers twice and gave her a full hysterectomy.

After that, my mum didn't finish a week without a couple of days in bed. I was kept off school to look after her. She was terribly unhappy and very ill. I wouldn't wish her life on anyone.

The years passed, and she perked up after divorcing my stepdad. She had a new doctor who injected life into her veins from a bottle: Guinness. Her new prescription was loaded with iron, which could have been the magic ingredient. For a while her energy returned; like me, she was always anemic.

Within a couple of years, we spoke sensibly to each other; her bitterness had dried. I was older and could hold an unemotional conversation. She enjoyed these times we had together, where we smoothed over some of the past. The last two years of her life, Alan and I helped her with house bills; she was unable to work or leave her bedroom. We were becoming friends, she started to compliment me, and even called me her daughter towards the end. Once she tried to cuddle me, but it was the most awkward moment, and I froze. I yearned to, but didn't feel time erased enough scars.

At 52, she was taken into hospital for the last time. Alan and I took turns visiting her every night for six months. She was always sitting up waiting for us and would relive her younger life. I was introduced to her world, and I loved it. On the 21st of December, I received a call; her heart gave up in the night during an asthma attack. I didn't react. I had no idea what I felt. My gran, her mum, had a stroke and died two weeks later. Then, a few months after that, my stepdad died of throat cancer. The floodgates opened as the people who raised me had gone within five months of each other. Three funerals to attend along with my babies, and I was choking up inside.

Over the years, I have thought about the three influences in my life: my stepdad, my gran, and my mum. For some reason, I won't hear a wrong word against my stepdad. I haven't mentioned his bad point—he was exceptionally violent when the drink took hold. But, the good in him was influential in sculpting me into the person I became. He undoubtedly injected me with the strength to cope with the future waiting for me.

* * * *

Running away became a favourite hobby of mine. Why stay indoors where the atmosphere was cold and chilly when I could delight in the sunshine and take part in adventures waiting for me?

It was probably after my visit to the chip shop that I realized there was a bigger game outside. Neighbors and passersby would often smile and wave at me where I sat, faced to the bay window. I would hide for hours inside the velvet curtain where no one from the house could find me. Like a wasp, walking up and down the glass, trying to escape to the other side, I wanted to fly, too. When I was strong enough to slip my weedy body over the chewed up wooden fence I was away. The fence was the springboard to my sanctuary.

I finger-trotted over the kitchen table for tasty bits of food and would stash them in my green Wellington boots. Even though I was young, I knew Micky and I would be out a long time and our bellies would be complaining if they didn't get fed. Sometimes Micky and I would run and hide among the bales of straw which resembled huts. After a few lazy hours, we would roam further until we reached the many shades of green foliage which was hanging from the trees. They draped their brown and gold branches towards me, and I would climb along them until I found a treasured spot as near to the top as I dared. Poking my head up to the blue forever, wanting to get even higher, I would keep my eyes wide open and breathe in the roaming clouds of uncertainty. Eventually, I would be brought back to reality with an earful of Micky's constant barking from below the tree where I had abandoned him.

Micky was always up for a runaway and would be out, hitting the road like a prisoner on the run. We would carry on sprinting until the houses were out of sight. The longest run we had together was a few days after my stepfather had brought me back home from a farmer's house in Leeds. The police had been looking for me for three days and my stepdad for longer. I hadn't yet started school and my mum, aided by my gran, thought it was wise to have me adopted. Years later, I had nightmares about a huge house with large ceilings and a golden chandelier hanging in the dining room that seemed to laugh at me with many glass eyes that changed color in the light. The memories of this brief time are vivid. Everything was rather grand and calculatingly placed, from the rich gold and red carpets to a china vase on the hallway table. My senses provoked me. Goosebumps sprouted on my arms and made the hair stand up as if my body was under attack from an old smell, not dirty or rotten, but a multitude of scents associated with unfinished conversations. Strange thoughts drifted in my head, and I could smell rose petals and violets all around the big bedroom where I was to live. I recognized a distinctive chill about the whole house, a spiritual decline.

There was a gentle teenage boy who talked to me as if we had a special bond, and although I didn't understand his words I understood their intent and his generous smile gazing down at me. He was the one who fed me, as I was reluctant to eat at the grand table where I had been scooped up. I was placed into chair so large I couldn't reach the arms and my legs were too short to dangle over the sides. He had me eating from his hand, pickled onions and crispy toast slightly burnt by the red-hot coals on the fire. His astute sensitivity latched onto my needs. Maybe he thought I was a fallen bird. I would have undoubtedly looked a sight with my tangled hair, knotted up with tears. When night came, I was placed in the middle of a big iron bed, and my uneasy sleeping patterns surfaced. My new family couldn't comprehend this behavior, and within a short time they let me go back where I came from.

The reaction from my stepdad and brothers showed I was missed. They surrounded me with laughter and joy. Even Micky contributed by wagging his tail profusely and waving a bone in front of me. I enjoyed the attention, but I looked for her, hoping for a reaction from my mum. She sat at the kitchen table, smoking a cigarette the smoke of which she blew my way. I believe that was her way of saying she missed me, too.

Over the years some of the village folk also thought it was in my best interest to be rehomed. Two families braved it and knocked on our door, asking if they could adopt me. I was close to both families, who I enjoyed spending time with. They had asked me many times if I would like to live with them, but I didn't understand what they meant and said no. Anyway, I couldn't leave Micky or my brothers to fend for themselves. My stepdad told the families, in no uncertain terms, to clear off.

Like every other time I ran, it was for no particular reason apart from I loved being outdoors and didn't enjoy being around my mum. Once, I had been studying the ground below me and became quite lost. The winter weather had hardened the ploughed fields. Weariness was settling on Micky and me, and I hadn't noticed the dark clouds before the rain was falling. Daylight was deserting us, and thunder and lightning swung around in the sky. Half a dozen horses, which had been frolicking around in a field, scattered, and I could only hear the roaring heavens above which frightened me from all logic. I had never seen the skies turn that way before.

We took refuge in a gutter. I threw myself into the bottom of the pit to ensure I was below ground level and curled up like a hedgehog, coated in mud, with Micky huddled on top of me. I don't remember what happened next until I was awakened by Micky's barking. My subconscious told me we had been disturbed. I was lying in semi-dark; cold liquid and the smell of rotten egg reminded me of a septic tank. Someone pulled at my clothes and lifted me out of the gutter. I felt warm arms around me but couldn't stir or open my eyes fully as the cold and wet had numbed my body.

Two days later I woke up in a strange little bed in front of an open fire. An elderly lady looked up at me from her cottage chair where she was knitting a red blanket square. After she watched me shuffle around the bed into a seated position, she walked over and asked my name.

Everything else happened unnaturally fast; I was eating some delicious homemade soup, cuddling up to Micky, who seemed quite at home, when a heavy knock disturbed us.

The petite lady let the wind and my stepdad in when she opened the back door. Apparently, he and some village folk, along with the police, had been searching everywhere for me. I did feel sorry for this man, who was always at work when I took my leave. I never wanted to worry him and couldn't understood why he was always so nice after he found me. He would just tut away at me, smiling, then gather me up into his arms. I'd cling to him like a limpet and bury my face in his chest while he whistled a tuneful melody all the way home. He often said I was descended from gypsies and sometimes I have thought that, too.

* * * *

When Mum had enough of us running under her feet, she would give us a punishment. It always seemed to be Alan and me; Alan because he was a nervous wreck, and me because it was me. The punishment she had carefully designed was to send us packing with orders not to come home until we had found a four-leaf clover. And with that statement, she would slam the front door in our little faces.

Patience was never my forte, but Alan could doodle and focus on the simplest things. He saved the day and found a good spot where shamrocks overruled the grass. It was a mammoth task, verging on impossible. The hours were cruel to us; we must have picked hundreds of three-leaf clovers. Guilt stationed in my mind because they curled up and died after we had rejected them, but we were homeless until we achieved our goal. We carried on like little soldiers, relentless, laughing and playing between serious moments. Micky brought a meatless bone which made us feel hungry.

The sky changed, indicating hours had passed and Alan, oblivious to everything, was still searching. He was so wrapped up in his task to find the elusive clover. I, on the other hand, was struggling to concentrate and offered my white body to the bright sun and the long grass. My stomach was frantically churning because I hadn't fed it since early morning and my energy was deserting me. I was just about ready to give up when Alan sweetly swept up my low mood and yelled in glee—he waved a tiny piece of green stuff with four round sides. I hesitated in disbelief. It was the real deal: a four-leaf clover.

After I brushed Alan's neck with kisses, making him giggle, we leapt up and kicked our legs like a couple of frisky colts welcoming the evening breeze. Yet we knew from experience that if we went home early, we'd be bundled up to bed. Eventually, we settled under the oak tree and waited for the day to finish.

My stepdad appeared from his workplace, and we danced behind him all the way home. This punishment came our way at least twice a year, and Alan always found the obscure four-leaf clover.

* * * *

I always had a love for critters, especially guinea pigs and rabbits. My stepdad bred the white fluffy things known as New Zealand whites for food and sold them to the village folk. Rabbit stew was considered a delicacy in our territory.

When I was big enough I was the rabbit keeper, a responsible position. I would rise early every morning and gather the rabbits to release them into wire-meshed runs, giving them the entire day to gobble up grass, clover, and dandelion leaves. They adored the leaves of dandelions more than any other; it is a nutritious weed, containing more beta-carotene than carrots. The yellow flowers sit above thick leaves, and their stems leaked a white milky substance that marked my clothes when I picked them.

After the treadmill of the school day, I would race home to see my furry friends and clean their hutches before carrying them back into their cozy beds for the night. This job could never be speeded up because I always wanted to talk to them about my long day. I thought they understood me and found them to be good listeners, though one rabbit was exceptional and touched my heart more than any other.

This rabbit always refused to leave the run when the day turned dim. She would play hide and seek most mornings when I was in a hurry to get her out of her cage. Her feet would stamp in defiance at me. I named her Suki against my stepdad's wishes; he had told me not to get attached.

Her stubborn naughtiness somehow delighted me. I found our relationship a pure delight, and over the two years we had together we developed a loving bond. After giving me a hard time, she would succumb if I started to pet another rabbit. Her jealousy made me laugh. She would jump herself forcefully on my knee, then I would put the other rabbit down for her.

Suki became tame and would sit on my lap while I dangled my legs on the wooden swing which hung from a tree at the end of our garden. She was a unique character, and the older she got the more her personality delighted me. Sometimes I would watch her tease Micky, who thought she was a smaller dog to play with; they would chase each other round the garden, until one of them got bored. Suki always outwitted Micky.

I lost her, and my heart took its first tumble. My tummy felt warm that night after eating my dinner. I excitedly asked permission to leave the table and said I wanted to see Suki before I went to bed. My Mum turned to me and said, 'You will have a job because you just ate her.' I jumped off my chair and ran outside into the garden and found her cage door wide open. I called her name over and over with tears racing down my face. My stepdad told me she was always intended for the table and I had been warned many times not to get attached.

After choking up inside, I vomited. The idea that I had eaten my little friend was just too much to bear. My stepdad, who had followed me into the garden, didn't say a word and walked away, leaving me to get over it. I threw myself on the garden swing and just rocked my body, making the strange humming sound which eased me. Micky lay close by in sympathy.

After that day, I refused to eat any rabbit, and the smell of it cooking makes me feel ill. I never understood why they would feed me my own pet, when they knew I loved her.

* * * *

I was the luckiest girl alive when my partner in crime, Micky, came to live with us. He was a cross between an Airedale terrier and an Alsatian. He did look a sight at first glance with his head and tail out of proportion to his puppy body, but his charisma and intelligence made him exceptionally adorable.

He boycotted the rest of my family and darted straight over to me. I was on the floor in my favorite corner, watching everyone flustering around him. I'm unsure why he sought me from the clan, but he opened my world. I was four and, like him, just getting my bearings. In no time, we were a Bonnie and Clyde in the making and would storm the village daily looking for entertainment. Sometimes Micky would pull me out of the scrapes I landed in because I was such an inquisitive kid. I'd wander to places I shouldn't, but he would be watching everyone who got too close. Micky strengthened my backbone.

One Saturday morning, Micky and I passed the butcher's van. He had pulled up outside his shop and opened his rear doors, ready to unload the meat which was sold already. However, the butcher was sidetracked by a customer.

Micky, not missing an opportunity, jumped into the back of the van and out again with a string of sausages hanging from his mouth. He ran past me with a guilty look in his brown eyes. My jaw dropped, and my eyes stretched beyond belief. The butcher and customers started shouting and chasing Micky, who was in big trouble. I sprinted past the lynch mob. I knew the red-faced butcher wouldn't have any kind words to say to me. I was used to running away from people, and in no time I was at the end of the village. Micky was a good 200 feet in front and all I could see was the sausages sweeping the road. I called, but the little chap was too frightened to turn back.

The butcher had run a lot further than anyone else, but his short legs and wide girth had brought him to a standstill. He was angry and breathless and shouting my name. I knew I'd be pulled over for this, so decided to stay away from the village until dark. After finding a tree to sit on I waited, knowing Micky was close. Once I relaxed, and the village folk had gone Micky walked over to me sheepishly. All I could see was a cute, cheeky pup and I stroked his head. Looking back to that day makes me laugh; how Micky outwitted the village butcher dragging behind him the long trail of sausages.

My partner in crime didn't die in my arms. Fate dished him a brutal death. It was Boxing Day; I hadn't noticed Micky had slipped away until a loud knock was heard at our front door. I was 12 at the time and felt the seriousness of the vibrations. When my stepdad opened the front door, a large pair of boots pressed mud onto our green hall carpet. It was the head huntsman from the Hall, who had often practiced his bad language on me and chased me off his owner's land. A couple of days prior he had threatened my dog. Micky had a soft spot for the females; he was trying to get around a bitch that was coming into heat. The huntsman had whacked Micky repeatedly with his riding whip and chased us both away.

Micky often disappeared when a bitch in season, even though I tried my best to keep him in. But as soon as my stepfather left the house, my mum would often send us both out for a walkabout.

The huntsman was fuming and told us that my dog was nothing but a nuisance, and he had thrown Micky over the high wire fencing where the hunting hounds were penned in. Micky was dead, they had ripped him literally apart. My stepdad's face wasn't pretty, but he accepted it with a stern nod.

I was in emotional turmoil and couldn't understand why they could be so flippant about my special friend. After the man left our house, my stepdad stood silently in front of the big hearth and turned away from me with his head low. I stood belligerent, staring at his back with silent tears choking me. The rest of the family remained at the kitchen table with not even the sound of clicking knives and forks.

I waited for him to turn around and look at me, but he didn't move. I went and sat back in my place at the table, now sobbing uncontrollably into the blue and white tablecloth which soaked up my tears. Finally, he stood above me and spoke my name in a serious tone. I raised my head and listened. He told me straight it was all my doing and if I had taken better care, Micky would still be alive. I accepted his verdict, knowing I introduced Micky to the hounds when we walked to the village green on Sundays. We enjoyed watching the huntsmen on horseback, dressed in their red and black coats with four brass buttons. They looked arrogantly regal and impressed a child wearing leftover clothes. I hadn't considered what they got up to, just the parade and excitement when the hunting horns stirred the hounds into a frenzy.

* * * *

Before I started secondary school, each morning my stepdad would come into my room and lift me up from a corner on the bedroom floor. I was like a little rocking horse, emotionless and in a trance, humming a strange tune. I started this bizarre behavior when I was a toddler, and it carried on for years until I felt safe enough to give up this coping mechanism. I wasn't aware I was upset about anything but found it hard to sleep because of nightmares. It was common for my long-suffering stepfather to rush in and wrap me tightly in a woollen blanket, and then he would hold me until my mind and body settled down. Eventually, he took me to see a doctor who concluded my imagination was too extreme for my age and reassured him I needed time to develop. I was labelled an introvert; I didn't like people much. I was often scolded by my mum for talking. Fortunately, school rectified this when I had to stand up for my three brothers. On reflection, it was likely I was going through trauma to behave the way I did because my night-time habits were always much worse when my parents had been fighting.

My behaviors increased when my heart hurt for my brother. There was a special treatment my brother Alan received, and when I say "special" I'm not referring to pleasantness. For years I witnessed Alan, who was a year younger than me, being stripped naked and pushed face down on a white linen bed. Then watch an unsympathetic nurse give him his early morning enema. His bowel problem began when he was around five years old and just started school. We children were never told what was going on, and incapable of understanding any of it, all we could see was our mum and the lady in a blue uniform doing something horrible to our brother. I can't imagine his physical and mental pain. His frightened, slight body would initially wrestle like a rabbit caught in a trap to escape the big hands settling down on him.

My mind couldn't deal with his sobbing and the way his big blue eyes dug into mine. I would sit cross-legged, rocking in the corner, silent tears would roam down my face, and I smudged my eyes many times with my crumpled sleeves. Unlike my other brothers, who would go into hiding until it was over, I couldn't desert him. I stayed in the room on alert, ready to jump up to hold Alan in my arms when the adults had finished this treatment. Once they left the room I rushed frantically to get him dressed, then, like magic, all would be forgotten, and we would be laughing outside as if nothing had happened.

Years later I understood more about this barbaric procedure. Alan had developed a blocked bowel, and the unwise doctor told my parents that he was just a lazy child and a few enemas would get his bowel working normally again. But they got it wrong, and by the doctor voicing his opinion it could be said he had given my parents a free license to punish my little brother even more.

A "good hiding" was what they called it from where I grew up. That often meant my stepdad would remove his leather belt or would bend me over his knee and slap aggressively until my face was as red and blotchy as my bottom. I cannot ever remember any of us little ones being naughty; we excelled at being invisible and silent and, if truth be told, I believe our parents assumed hitting a child was normal and regarded it as beneficial therapy.

Luck never found time for Alan, and his primary school experience was not pleasant. The Head Teacher treated him as if he had mental disabilities, and when he had finished humiliating Alan, the school children would willingly jump like a pack of hyenas waiting for the kill. Alan stationed himself around me as much as he was allowed, and I did everything I could to keep him safe. I only had the power of a child, but it was enough to keep other children away.

Ironically, once Alan started secondary school his problem just went away. He had a nice, gentle teacher. She read between the lines and probably compared us kids as a family lot because we all had been affected by our household in different ways. Thankfully, time is a great healer and children are resilient; we kept climbing back up like persistent spiders.

When Alan left school his only side effect was low self-esteem and nervousness, which dominated his personality. But after a few years, he cleverly ironed out his childhood memories and moved forward to embrace a positive life.

* * * *

Anthony's school life was no better. He looked the double of his dad which gave him no brownie points. The Head Teacher hated my stepfather. I never knew why, but he often brought his name up when referring to middle-class society, where my stepfather rooted from. It was obvious, even to a little girl, that this teacher had a chip on his shoulder. The teacher was a self-made man; he would rattle on about his difficult army days and how he had to drag himself out of a pit of poverty and fight to get an education. His theory of success was to follow a strict code of discipline, and punishments were a vital part of education and growth at my school. We children never needed these sermons, as his daily actions left us in no doubt at all.

My stepfather, on the other hand, had come from a more affluent, relaxed background. He had received a privileged education. He was also blessed with "Dirk Bogarde looks", an English actor who broke many a lady's hearts in the film, *A Doctor in the House*. My stepdad also had ladies vying for his attention when we went to the shops. My neck would be craning over my shoulder, not wanting to miss a trick; they were like freshly turned vampires sighting their first kill. However, he only had eyes for one woman, my mum.

The primary school ticked away like clockwork, with all the teachers and children guided by the over- accelerated rule system electrified by one man. Everyone seemed to walk cautiously around the Head, who took delight sieving out the weak and timid child to belittle. On these frequent occasions, he would pull a chosen victim to the front of the class and bellow down into their small face until they cried. His temper was always flaring up like a burgundy rash. Then he would march around the classroom, physically poking the children from side-to-side without any regard for their feelings.

One day, Anthony was dragged from his wooden desk and made to stand against a wall, his crime unknown. The Head was shouting more viciously than normal, and we were all confused. My eyes were glued to his every move. After a few minutes, he got tired of listening to his own arrogant voice and changed tactics. He curled his sinewy arms around Anthony's head and boxed him in before he pulled his locks down against his chest. He hadn't finished yet and launched Anthony head and body against the wall.

The sound that followed could only be described as a hard-boiled egg being cracked against a plate. The class didn't breathe. What looked like red paint ran down Anthony's face, and I bolted up and cried out. My body was flaring like a little firecracker when I ran and placed myself in front of my brother. I tried to match the teacher's screaming.

My short arms crossed in front of my face when I tried to pull him away from my brother. The teacher let his hands drop then studied me for as long as it would take to flick a page in a book. His eyes were full of craziness. I stood there, showing no emotion apart from teardrops indicating the pain I felt for Anthony. The teacher just walked away.

I turned to Anthony, who was weeping, and I let his head drop to my chest, which gave him some comfort. I tried to force Anthony to leave the room with me, but he refused. I watched his tears watering down the blood that was sliding through his albino hair and tugged at him to follow me, but he couldn't move. The whole class seemed to be of the same mindset; it was as if everyone had been turned into stone apart from me.

I called to my younger brother, Alan, in a forceful voice to come with me. He was only eight years old but he jumped up, causing his chair to fly across the floor. Still, the other children didn't react; they were trapped in their own fear.

I took Alan's hand, and we both scampered out of the room. We met my stepdad on the way home; he was returning to work after his lunch and must have noticed something was wrong, because he sprinted towards us. I spouted off my version of events before we even got close, but he had taken in every word. He placed his hand on my shoulder. After my breathing was normal, he told a work colleague to send the police up to the school then sent young Alan home.

I went back to school with him.

We strode into class confidently, side-by-side. I loved those moments of unity between us. Our senses were sharp. The class was now working quietly under a young teacher's instruction. She looked quite embarrassed when she saw us. She took us to the school nurse, who had just finished bandaging Anthony's head. My brother stood up smiling in relief and happy to see us. My stepdad told us to wait outside the school gate. He went back to find the Head Teacher.

We walked out holding hands and waited dutifully for our protector to return. After a while, all three of us walked home tight-lipped and the incident was not mentioned again. Anthony never returned to that school, nor did Alan for a long time. I wanted to go back straight away. The following week I walked into the classroom, and the whole incident had been whitewashed. No one mentioned the incident until the close of day, when the Head called me to his office. He spoke to me as if I was a fully-understanding adult; he always did, maybe because I wasn't timid and afraid like most kids. He made a big point of telling me that my stepdad wasn't a part of me. I didn't know what he meant, and knew it was wiser to stay quiet.

* * * *

I was into my last year of primary school. The days had gone relatively smoothly after my encounter with the Head Teacher and the incident with Anthony. The leaves from the trees were curling, changing color, and falling like confetti. Underfoot the ground felt rough and unfriendly, a perfect condition for character building with cross-country running. All the 11-year-olds had to participate; the Head himself was at the forefront, giving us encouragement by waving a conductor's stick. This ensured we were more afraid of him than the four-mile runs.

Sport was one of my best subjects, and I finished second overall on Sports Day for two consecutive years. This disappointed me and I cried out of frustration, knowing the only reason I never won was because of a girl I was paired with in the three-legged race. She was known as the "left-over girl". No one chose her because she had no natural ability or inclination to take part. We wouldn't even get three steps without her falling over or giving up, but I never thought of asking her to try. She was a nice person, and didn't allow the bullies to get to her. I admired her for that.

My only weakness in sport was my fear of heights. Every Friday afternoon was scheduled for our cross-country run, regardless of weather conditions and excuses. I was the fastest runner in the school at the time and loved the challenge. My adrenaline would pump my blood, and I would sprint as if my life depended on it... until I spotted the swing bridge. Once there, my confidence would evaporate, and the rest of the class would overtake me.

The base of the bridge was strapped together by unmatched wooden planks which refused to lay still and made a creaking sound. Between these planks, there was no denying what was at the bottom: fast-moving, shiver-inducing waters. On a windy day, the bridge danced around clumsily.

The abuse started with an ear bashing from the Head Teacher. He carefully selected words intended to humiliate me in front of the class, apparently to make me a stronger person. I longed to have the courage to walk across the unsteady planks to the other side of the river, but I was like a racehorse that faulted at the last hurdle.

I looked at the bridge. It was my enemy. The teacher snatched my body up and dragged me to the middle of the bridge where he dropped me like a sack of spuds. Fear and relief came together, but my eyes were already closed as I was curling my body slowly like a worm until I was in a fetal position. I was deaf to the abusive words now. Eventually, he pulled me across the bridge to solid ground, where he released his hold and walked back to the school. The class hesitated a few seconds to acknowledge me, then jumped into single line behind the Head Teacher and followed his lead. I waited near the bridge until they were out of sight then walked backed with a heavy load on my mind.

CHAPTER THREE

To this day I can't recall any part of the accident, only what I've been told.

I landed on the concrete floor at the bottom of the stairs in my home. My legs and body were twisted over my head in a complex way. I was living in Bishop's Frome, Herefordshire at the time, and neighbors had heard a high-pitched scream which brought them immediately 'round. My children, having scrambled out of their beds when they heard the crash, were wandering around my body looking confused and frightened. Blood from my head injury had spurted onto the plastered walls. My neighbours Wendy and Bobbie said it was a moving sight to witness with the small children staring at my body like little white ghosts.

My surgeon, Mr. Steel, said my injury was not a loose fall, what he called "normal". I had finished a long day in the office, then played with the children, causing me to be overly tired. His opinion, backed by many years of medical experience, was that it was possible someone had been in the house at the time. He went on to say it was more plausible that I had been physically lifted and thrown into the air for my body to land in that strange position which caused my unique injuries.

What I didn't know at the time was that the front door lock had been smashed open and the neighbor who found me had called the police, who confirmed the door had been broken from outside. There was no sign of anyone lurking about, and nothing appeared to have been stolen from my home, but I was in no position to clarify.

Strangely, I have never remembered any part of it, during and after it happened. Even now, I still cannot remember the fall. My last recall was when I stood at the top of the stairs, peeking through a badly painted bedroom door listening to Nicole, sucking on her pink thumb in her cot. She had a glossy smile running across her cherubic face, which encouraged me to linger. A cold silence touched me whole! It felt like a dark blankness was consuming me from within, then something had gone badly wrong as if someone had turned off a switch in my brain. I wasn't alive as we know it; my body light and energy dissipated, and I was simply not there anymore.

Later, after I was taken into hospital, parts of my body started to wake up, and it was reported I was laughing loudly and singing in the middle of the night, causing quite a disturbance. I was hallucinating with the morphine drip swimming through my veins to kill the pain. This medication gave me a trip of a lifetime. For once, my quiet temperament did a somersault. I had no inhibitions, and my forthright Northern roots were illuminated when I argued with staff about wanting to go home. Colors, lights, and floating faces were all around me. Kind faces from my past and what felt like my parents' past. Bodies were blanketing my whole frame, their eyes were like torch lights all over my body, feeding me warmth. I could see flowers with large green and red leaves floating above me in the glowing sunshine.

This was my encounter on drugs, but they worked their magic and pulled me down to a resting place, enabling my nerves, muscles and, more importantly, my brain, to stop racing before it crashed into overdrive. I was struggling to make sense of what had happened, but there simply wasn't any.

The drawn-out days in my hospital bed were oppressively boring; minutes felt like hours and hours turned into weeks. I felt like Sleeping Beauty, but there was no prince on a white charger coming to my rescue. I yearned to remember what had happened to me and struggled to think, but it was useless. Every day my head was churning around like a dishwasher with clattering and drumming sounds, abusing my eardrums. This, along with unyielding migraines, overrode any common sense my cognition could muster.

I listened to my tentative doctor dishing words of wisdom and eventually agreed: in my case, it was better for me not to know what had happened. He felt it was too much for my mind to handle considering that I had been launched to hell and back and had a lot of challenges to face. My head was cut open; I had suffered a concussion, a moderate trauma, and it was hoped I would remember my accident within 24 hours. But my memory never returned.

After my trauma, my body and mind were not the same again. I noticed, and years later friends informed me, that I had a unique way of thinking and reacting to situations. The general opinion was that I had a personality shift. It was nothing to worry about, not as extreme as Jekyll and Hyde. Nevertheless, there was a significant difference.

My doctor in Hereford hospital spoke about this; he took the time and explained how the brain works. On a diagram, he pointed to where my head had been cut open, saying, 'Imagine your brain as an engine room with different railway lines taking messages all around your body, back and forth. Then something happens, and the lines crash together. You are left with some tracks broken, which means some information will not be delivered or received.'

Although we were relaxed in cool laughter, it was a serious, scary moment. Silence filled our space for some time before he hurriedly said, 'But in your case, your creative side of the brain will be accelerated, and you will be full of new inventive ideas.'

He was trying to soften the blow, of course. Obviously, at that time, neither of us knew how my mind and body were going to adapt to the changes. He rounded the conversation off cleanly, after searching my bloodless face and said, 'You will be quirky, interesting, and unique, and no one will ever know you had a head injury.' That did help to put me at ease as I was starting to think I would be considered a fruit loaf. I laughed with him and to myself, thinking most of my life random people have labelled me as an arty, dreamlike character anyway. You see, before my accident, I was exceedingly creative, musically, and artistically. I could draw anything as a child and loved pottering with any art and craft materials I could get my hands on.

My surgeon's confidence in me was later reinforced when he came to say goodbye. He told me I was one of the most inspirational patients he had met and said he had many macho men pass through his hands who had half my health problems and they just gave up the fight. He offered me a job working for him in his office, which made me hoot with laughter; I was incapable of counting or staying on a topic of conversation. But I couldn't have wished for a more dedicated and thoughtful doctor standing by my side.

* * * *

Panic attacks and random sweating episodes frequently soaked my body and hair, as if the dial controlling the temperature on a boiler had been turned onto high and was flying out of control. Side effects occurred more when I was anxious and frightened for myself and my children in everyday life situations. They would go together with my debilitating migraines. I would be vomiting periodically for days until my body settled down. Before the life-changing accident, I couldn't have comprehended how painful and immobilizing a migraine could be.

These specific side effects escalated when I could leave my house and start mixing within the community again; within the confinements of home I felt safer, and when my children were around they took control. These little people never panicked or cried, but would sit on the floor for hours with me, bathing my head with hot or cold facecloths, depending whether my body temperature was high or low.

Oh, how I loved when my children were teenagers. They were a comfort and a blessing. Once they left home, I had a reality shock. It seemed as though the lights in the house went dim and I had to learn to cope with invisible disabilities all over again. I had not realized how much my children had looked after me.

One day, I was put to rights by my eldest, Luke, when he sat me down and said, 'Mum, you need to get yourself together.' I looked puzzled and asked him what he meant. He replied, 'Well, your behavior changes daily, depending on your confidence. One day you refuse to let us open the curtains, and you ask us to pull the phone lead out because you are frightened to speak to people. Then another day, you will lose something, such as a pen, and spend the whole day fixed on it even though the reason you wanted it had long gone.'

I was rocked by the astute observations from my son. His word was absolute and I, too, noted how odd my behavior was. I often couldn't remember what I said to people, including the children, within seconds. I had to get a healthier mental control. Otherwise, the wrong person would jump to the wrong conclusion and have me sectioned as a madwoman.

At times, I would come across as the dopey female who would amuse others, but inside I wanted to scream because I knew I was not pretending. I was struggling to do mundane tasks, such as looking at the date in a diary or writing an appointment on the calendar. I couldn't process information. I was petrified in case I was mislabelled and diagnosed with a form of dementia. I had given this considerable thought and researched for many hours until I made the decision to find the key to unlock the damaged parts of my brain. I understood that with any brain injury you should push yourself to learn, and if one strategy doesn't work try another, even if it seems futile at the time. Eventually, I took a degree in Inclusive Learning to learn more about myself and individuals with unique disabilities. I wanted more insight and innovative ideas to help me adapt to the new me. I took this degree in conjunction with a part-time teaching job at a primary school, Early Years Foundation Stage. At that time, I was not capable of teaching at a higher level but needed to get some confidence back.

Eventually, I did develop a normal daily routine comparable to other working mothers, but it took time and perseverance. I set about re-training myself. I wrote a minute-by-minute account of my daily routines and kept re-reading my notes. Even elementary reading was difficult; I was exceedingly slow and would painstakingly read aloud like a five-year-old child and often missed words. An important part of this self-designed personal therapy approach was accepting all my limitations gracefully without feeling inadequate.

Time worked with my body and mind, and soon I felt a stronger person but was afraid of people. I knew they only had to say a negative word or look at me in a certain way to knock my confidence. I joined a class on assertive behaviour, however, I refused to speak throughout all the sessions. But I left the house, which was a start. Later, I tried again and enrolled in a counselling course to challenge myself. This was more successful, and I gradually came out of my shell once realizing no one was perfect, and other people had their own issues to deal with. I studied Floristry at Pershore College, renowned for its excellent reputation, which ignited my creative spark again. I excelled in floral design, and within a few months, thanks to a friend named Cally, people were knocking at my door wanting flower arrangements.

* * * *

Cally delighted in my floral work, and when she wanted a bouquet she called me. Initially, I believed she was just super kind until she introduced me to a work colleague who asked me to organize her daughter's wedding flowers. This turned out to be a rather grand affair. I relished the challenge, having free creative range.

Cally worked for the Social Services Department when we met. I was at my lowest edge the morning I walked off the street and into her office with one objective: to give away my children. Winter was chewing on my bones, and I couldn't walk more than a few half-steps without my back going into spasms. Every lamp post and brick wall allowed me minutes to reboot my energy to keep going. The children, though small, were my walking supports.

For many years Christmas was painful for me. Not being able to purchase a tree was too much. Georgia kept asking for a pretty fairy; I knew first-hand what it was like not to have what other children had and didn't want my babies to be left out.

We were living in Malvern, and Cally's office was close by. The double door was hard to open, but the children and I pushed together. Straight away I was encouraged to sit. I knew I had an opaque, lifeless look about me and needed the seat urgently.

I told Cally I couldn't take anymore and broke down, pitifully whimpering. It was a dizzy moment for us all; I was rushed through a private door and served tea, which warmed me. After I had gathered my decorum, I churned out how I felt. Cally and a young colleague listened intently and guided my words into other corners of my life until she held a clear picture in her mind. It was obvious she cared. I found it easy to be open with this lady. Interestingly, strangers often make the best listeners.

After giving Cally chapter and verse, I explained a day didn't go by without excruciating back pain topped often with migraines. I spoke about my inadequate parenting skills. At the time, I assumed I wasn't good enough because I couldn't buy the children treats and new clothes, but Cally wasn't having any of it; her people skills were razor-sharp. She hesitated and studied my well-behaved chicks clinging to me and asked them their names; she made it easy and knelt at their height. Their little faces churned into bubbles of smiles. They knew they were safe.

Cally concluded nothing was wrong with me or my parenting skills, and she wanted to help. I told her the doctors had suggested my problems were all in my head, and they used the single mother card for my struggle to cope. That was because my new doctors hadn't seen my previous medical notes. They had been lost during transit when we moved from Bishop's Frome in Herefordshire to Malvern, Worcestershire.

After that day, Cally put together a support plan for me and enrolled my children in a Young Careers group which allowed them to go on day trips and outings with other children. They needed to be children, not nursemaids.

* * * *

A marvellous opportunity presented itself when I was asked to decorate the stage for a production of the musical, *The Secret Garden*. My own daughter, Georgia, was given the lead part of Mary. With help from everyone in the production, we decorated the stage with an abundance of vibrant flowers and wild foliage. I got up early that morning to plunder the forgiving woods for long strands of ivy and assortments of contrasting green leaves which I needed in my arrangements. My children enjoyed the rushed excitement in raiding the woodlands. I was touched with guilt for taking from nature but reminded myself I was making room for new growth. I'm sure I must have looked like a bag lady with the black bin bag I was dragging across the field towards the car with my people doing the same. It was such fun, and to me the children resembled high-spirited fairy folk.

Within a few hours of pleasurable work, the tired stage was transformed into a Garden of Eden. Ivy draped down the velvet curtains, ceilings, and archways. The stage had been transformed into an oasis of voluptuous intertwining greens, spotted with pink and yellow roses—simply alluring. When opening night came, the lights didn't stop bouncing across the stage while the curtains teasingly infolded to reveal the stage performers, including my two girls. They both enjoyed musical productions. Georgia just adored singing, and Nicole loved to dance.

It was becoming obvious that having children was not a hindrance but a blessing, and these half-pints aided my recovery as my motivators, my world. Although at times we struggled to cater to basic needs, we managed. Twice I was informed by doctors that I was suffering from malnutrition, but there was nothing to be done with limited funds. I worked, looked after my children, rested when able, and was happy.

Life got better. I started mixing more in public and going to craft fairs on weekends. I was a pyrography artist, and joined associated Craft Guilds by invitation. Although I couldn't lift the boxes of wooden items out of the van alone, my children didn't mind how many times they trotted back and forth to fetch one or two items at a time until the boxes were empty, and we were able to set up our stall. They thrived on the attention customers and stall holders gave them. By the end of the day, their bubbly personalities earned them a few coppers or something tasty from stall holders. My artwork had introduced us to a vibrant community. This opportunity helped my children develop their social skills, which escalated on Monday mornings when they tripped over their tongues in excitement to tell their teachers about their weekends.

I received extra work via commissions. Members of Women's Institutes loved my pyrography and booked me to give talks at their local community hall. The money was nice and needed. Most of my earnings came from pet portraits or house signs. Running up to Christmas got unmanageable at times with orders of flower and candle arrangements and bespoke pyrography orders, but I enjoyed the buzz and the feeling of worth. It was refreshing to be around lovely people, especially the older generation, who had the time to bestow their wisdom on my children.

It was never my idea to become a public speaker. I was shy, reserved, and the thought would never have occurred to me. In the beginning, I was excited to give my first talk. The ladies in the Women's Institutes are highly intelligent and outwitted all my attempts to excuse myself. I needed to be coaxed out of my shell, though. Once I had survived my suspenseful, unprepared audition, I felt liberated and got into the swing of openly talking to strangers about my crafts, chiefly pyrography. Each piece of wood is unique before it has been crafted. I never had a client who wasn't happy with their finished commission. This was immensely rewarding, and looking back I realize it was therapy for me. The children benefited, too. We had gone from hiding behind curtains and sitting in the dark to publicly demonstrating and flashing our designed crafts in an attempt to bring in the pound. After my accident, I believed my only purpose was to recover and raise my children, hoping they would grow into well-rounded, caring individuals and, at times, I wasn't sure I would see them grow up. After that, I assumed my body would pack up and die. Wasn't I in for a shock? My children went from being nervous and shaky to confident. They also became knowledgeable in many areas. Nicole, at 14, would happily pass the time with a ladies group if I was detained for some reason. The ladies seemed to enjoy her company and would congratulate me as Mum afterwards. After a time, my children had the flair to sell anything and insisted on making their own items to sell, like wooden key rings and bookmarks, which provided them with pocket money for the first time. They played for hours with their hard-earned cash before deciding whether to spend or save.

I'll never forget a perfect English summer day, when we went on an outing to the seaside, Weston Super Mare. It was the first time my children had seen the sea and sand. We were rounded up like lambs and helped onto the mini-bus organized by our local church. My children always enjoyed Sunday school and, like me, they adored the hymns and the ambience afterwards when refreshments were being served and the congregation buzzed in vibrant conversation.

I wasn't walking properly at the time but was seated on a dream coat blanket folded over the sand. I felt my children's happiness; their excited eyes were glancing everywhere. A friend had made us a picnic basket full of surprises. I relaxed with Nicole cuddled between my knees. We watched the older children and adults playing volleyball. It was such an easy day full of fun and laugher. After some time, I missed the bright voices of my little people. I failed to notice Joe and Georgia had drifted away from view. Usually, they would stay within sight, but they had been chasing a colorful beach ball.

I panicked and was calling out their names, which made Nicole cry, feeding off my anxiety. A young couple from our church came over and told me not to worry, they would find my children while I stayed with Nicole. Ten minutes passed before I could relax again when I heard Georgia's harmonious laughter heading my way. I looked up to see them, hand-in-hand, running towards me. Georgia's big blue eyes were sparkling like balls of glitter, and Joe looked sheepish before he let go of his sister's hand and pushed her in front of me.

Their faces were smothered with ice cream, and chocolate was rolling down their chins, dribbling over their snowy white T-shirts. I laughed as Joe gave me an ice lolly which had been lying in his plastic bucket.

I asked him who had bought the treats. Joe replied with confidence and said 'Mummy, you have no money. I lifted Dordie (Joe always called Georgia "Dordie") up onto a big rock and told her to sing like Annie from the musical while I walked around shaking my bucket at people. They gave us lots of money.' He said it as if it was a normal occurrence; I felt guilty and wanted to cry realizing this seven-year-old understood money was fundamental to existence. I had unintentionally drilled it into them not to ask for things because we had no money. I thought, how naive of me not to think my children wouldn't notice what other children had, and of course, want ice cream at the beach. Although, I did always remind them we have something a lot of families don't have: an abundance of love, with fun and laughter.

I looked into the bucket and was stunned. A pot of gold and silver, the bucket was half-full of coins shining in the sunshine. Joe handed his little red bucket to me and said, 'Mummy, we can buy bread and milk now.' Bread and milk, those words rolled off my tongue daily in our house. My head was taken down after I studied his serious face; it was obvious he was proud, knowing he had done something grand. This little man, who should want for nothing, was thinking up ideas to feed his family.

I explained to them both that I didn't want them to do it again and said the money could be spent on greater things. I called the vicar over and suggested a donation towards the church roof. She got my drift and winked before kneeling to make eye contact with Joe. Georgia was totally oblivious to the whole conversation, as she was having a wonderful time with her first taste of coned ice cream. Although Joe was only a year older it was obvious he had other ideas, and thought it was his hard-earned cash. After juicy words from the vicar, he reluctantly let her pull his bucket away. I thought he was going to cry. There was a silver lining to this story when, a week later at church, Joe was called up and presented with a starred certificate in his name. When everyone clapped in appreciation, he must have grown inches.

The outing at the seaside became a once-yearly affair; a chance to regroup and laugh and play with each other. It was a release with blue open skies and the sea casting as far as sight allowed. The children would be thrashing around, playing on the sand, stretching their bodies until daylight drained their youthful energy and would bring them back to my open arms.

This alone was my reward. I'd sit and breathe in the fresh air while watching their small faces and hear their sweet laughter while they were being guided by nature. People from the church were virtually strangers, though they were kind and jolly. Strangers were the best people for me to be around after my accident. They appeared to find us an interesting lot; we didn't give much away. If someone pushed or wanted to dissect I would clam up and turn my face away.

* * * *

Once I was working full time again I secured a Victorian house overdosed with character and potential. The day we moved into our house in Malvern, Worcestershire I fell in love with its charm. It had stood empty for years and had a melancholy feel about it. I thought it could have been waiting for me, two lonely souls in different skins. I knew my children would inject their pure life force into the cold bricks and mortar.

This skeleton of a house, with fiercely stripped pine doors and a stairway half painted with orange paint, appealed. The old décor was a job crudely done. I was going to make this house whole again and transform it into a show home. My heart was placed, but I was under no illusion that it was going to be an easy job. It needed a damp course, rewiring, a new central heating system, then plastering. Before any job could be started, we needed to empty the house. The previous owner had been an elderly lady who had got lost in it for years before she had been taken into assisted living, leaving all her treasured memories. We found boxes and boxes of old newspapers, and it took three large skips over a six-week period before it was clutter-free. We took it a day at a time. It had a solid roof, spacious rooms, a large

Victorian garden, and light in abundance. We couldn't have been happier.

I made it a fun task with the children; we agreed every time we ventured outside the front door we would take something out to the skip. One Saturday, my back pain kept me in bed for most of the day. After dozing on and off, I heard voices. I called out but received no reply. Carefully, I made my way downstairs; the journey felt like it took forever as I clung to every wall and door handle to steady myself. When I finally reached the bottom, I noticed that the front door was wide open and on the path was a blanket displaying my worldly goods: pictures, pottery, handbags, and shoes, among other miscellaneous pieces my kids could find. Joe was securing a sale, and Georgia was eating some sweets. (I had no idea how she got them.) An old dinner set was about to find a new home when I intervened and told the customers that the sale was over and asked the children to bring everything back into the house.

I didn't say anything negative to my children; they were trying to help and were sick of basic, boring, cheap food. I admired their initiative; Joe handed me over £20.00. I was astonished when Richard, the greengrocer, came across and said I should be proud of my kids. They had been bartering like professionals, and all the locals came over to talk to them. I let the children choose what they wanted for tea that night and trusted Joe to go to the co-op around the corner with the £20.00 note and a twinkle in his eye.

* * * *

I was in less of a hurry to do things; I struggled deeply to make decisions, and nothing seemed relevant enough to pull me out of a daydream state. (This couldn't have been attributed to drugs because I refused to take any after I came out of hospital). Since my accident, I knew nothing could be rushed or forced anymore; my life flowed through me on its own time. Naturally, I knew I had limited abilities, but struggled to find the energy to fill the day. The burning pain at night ensured I didn't sleep through. With silent tears, I would rock myself to sleep. I played the smiling mum in front of the children. Otherwise, they would cry and ask me what was wrong. I needed to keep them positive. When my children felt confident enough to go back to their own beds I still struggled to sleep. I continued rocking my body from side to side, until exhaustion overrode the burning pain and I fell asleep. Each morning my sheet and pillows would be on the floor; it was even common for me to have switched bed ends completely while my body would be grinding away like a set of teeth.

* * * *

My first big fear, after becoming fully conscious again, was my speech. I couldn't speak correctly, my words were slurred, and some wouldn't surface, although I heard them in my mind. This frightened me witless; it was as if I'd had a mini-stroke. Mercifully this didn't last, and within a couple of weeks I was stringing sentences together. Occasionally I struggled to form a full sentence and missed connecting words. My mind would cut out, people noticed, as if a battery had run out mid-conversation. A dear friend, Jackie, picked up on this straight away and said it was more apparent when I hadn't eaten. After her astute revelation I ate small amounts often, and the issue only came back if I was extremely anxious about something.

When I was ready to walk, I discovered a weakness in my left knee and ankle. Dr. Peter Ngs and Dr. Steel previously revealed the left side of my body was weaker, primarily due to nerve damage, though the examinations stopped at the base of my spine. I walked a little, although my knee and ankle often hurt, which caused me to fall.

Dr. Ngs put a silk scarf evenly around my neck and asked me to walk across a room on a white line painted onto the floor. The scarf slid down my left side within a few steps. I cried, knowing at the time my shoulders were unbalanced. I couldn't stay upright no matter how hard I tried. My knee and ankle pained me for years and, even now, if I don't keep up the walking, my muscles get weak and my left ankle slips.

* * * *

After my diagnosis, doctors told me to get a wheelchair. They said it was unlikely I would ever be able to walk properly again. I was taken aback. I knew I was in a sorry state but didn't anticipate that outcome. There was no way I was going to accept such a cruel verdict. My small children needed me, and I had to work again to pay my bills and give my children a normal childhood.

While in hospital, my children were forced apart and taken into care unbeknownst to me. I had no family who could step in. My youngest child, Nicole, was only 18 months. I had absolutely no knowledge about this. At the beginning, I was totally disabled, in a clinical hospital bed with a neck brace, unable to move my body apart from my eyes. Any slip of movement rendered me in excruciating pain, leaving me reliant on others for all my needs.

Old friends from the past were unaware of my plight, due to my recent relocation, and now I was too laid up to get in touch with them. I studied the ceiling and changing light; it was my main view for a long time. The fluorescent light would flicker for ages, undecided if wanted to stay on or die until a nurse played with the switch. Thinking didn't really happen; I couldn't feel anything, and I didn't care.

A positive change came when my health visitor, Avril, visited seven weeks later and told me some vital facts: my children had been separated, had no knowledge of each other or whether I was alive or dead. My heart was cut out of me, then my blood boiled angrily. It hadn't occurred to me the vulnerable position they were in. I calculated all options and knew if I didn't pull myself out of this maze of fog and get out of hospital, my children's whole future stood in jeopardy.

This change in me delighted my doctor, who had grown anxious because my body wasn't healing. There was still a four-inch hole in my head that was not closing. My immune system had taken the lead from my mind and fallen asleep. But now I had to leave my deathbed and fight to get my family back. Within a week, the hole in my head was healing, I was eating everything in sight, and my body went into repair mode.

I still felt strange movements inside my head and thought there must be a brain tumor at work. This unpleasant feeling lasted nearly 11 months before it literally stopped overnight. My doctor said my body was remarkably healing itself.

* * * *

I went home much earlier than Hereford hospital wanted. I needed to be reunited with my children, and I nagged the hospital staff until they gave in. I knew they were thinking of my needs, but I had to consider my children's. The longer a child is in care, the harder it is for a parent to get their child back. All the time I was in the hospital I only saw my toddler, Nicole, once when the neighbor kindly brought her to see me. No one brought my other children in to check if their mummy was alive.

The last time they saw their mummy I was laid out, twisted on the concrete floor, covered in blood. My little one had walked all around me, crying and confused. She climbed onto my chest to stare into my face and played with my eyelids, trying to wake me up. I was unconscious; who knows what their little minds were thinking, especially since they were at a critical age of development.

I was worried and frantic when I realized that my children were not with qualified foster parents. And to make things worse, they had been separated from each other. A social worker had been brought in after my accident and had made the terrible decision to ask surrounding neighbors if they would take in my children. She said later, this was because she was trying to save the government money. She didn't check the neighbors' histories or go through correct channels. I didn't even know these people because I had recently moved to the area. It turned out the families were under the impression they were going to be paid. After I came home, I did get friendly with the couple that looked after Nicole. They were wonderful to her, treated her like their own little girl, and were a great support to me. My children had been emotionally traumatized. They were quite disturbed and insecure and wouldn't leave my side or let go of each other's hands once we were back together. My little son Joe, age five, had become aggressive and angry and was fighting at school. His four-year-old sister, Georgia, had begun sleepwalking every night. Three times a week at least she screamed and cried with nightmares. It was frightening, more so when she would stand at the top of the stairs in a trance-like state, attempting to jump. I bought a stair gate and had it fitted at the top of the stairs. Joe was permanently on the lookout for his sister. Nicole was bed-wetting for a long time even when she was at school; she suffered from panic and breathing attacks for years. I believe she had watched me too closely and mimicked my unhealthy habits. We all slept cuddled up tightly in my double bed at night- time. They couldn't be separated from me, or each other, for a long time until they fully understood that Mummy would never leave them again. Sadly, that is what they thought, that I had left them. They often asked *why* I left, which was painful to hear. I couldn't explain.

* * * *

It was agreed that I needed to be home, even though I hadn't yet had any physical therapy. While I was in hospital, I was rotated on a speciality bed. Periodically throughout each day, the staff would hoist it up at different angles. I could see in front of me and urinate through a catheter; this was the extent of my disability. I hadn't tried to walk or even been lifted into a chair and experienced the normal sitting position because my back wouldn't straighten up at this stage and that is why the hospital staff believed it was too early for me go home.

When the taxi driver came to collect me from the hospital, he couldn't lift me into the car because of my body position. He called for a larger vehicle to take me home and realized I had four steps to get over before reaching my front door. Two men had to carry me, afraid to even try to put me on the floor because I was terribly weak and frail-looking. I was lifted and carefully positioned like a broken china doll onto the homely settee. I felt sorry for the men; you could see they didn't want to leave me like that. Thankfully, the neighbor Wendy, who was looking after Nicole, walked in and stood, temporarily shocked, witnessing my situation. Wendy first told the men she would sort it out, then rushed back outside to get her husband, Bobby. He went upstairs and brought my bed down for me. They brought a commode, a walking frame, and bags of food.

They stayed, holding my hands until the social worker walked in with my children. This was pure magic for everyone in the room; screaming, crying, and a sense of ultimate relief smothered us all. I cried for the first time in months, not because of any persistent pain. I was just overjoyed to see their tiny faces again.

Every school morning a knock would come to the back door; it was a black taxi to take my children to Breakfast Club before school started. I was unable to leave the bed, and incapable of preparing breakfast or even make me a cup of tea. We relied on helpers. After school, the taxi would bring my little family home quite late. This was our normal daily routine; because they joined after-school clubs where they could play, take part in extracurricular activities, and enjoy a cooked evening meal. This was a great relief for me; I didn't have to worry about them, and I had more resting and sleeping time. While my body was in repair mode, I was physically and mentally exhausted for a long time. This only happened because of good friends all chipping in to ensure my children didn't miss out, and it was better for them not to spend too much time around me when I couldn't get out of bed and often showed signs of depression.

When they came home after a long day at school, my heart soared as they marched towards me. They were always excited to see me and threw their arms like one giant octopus around me. I would dive into their school bags to hunt for pictures and written work they had produced. They would happily line up to read with me before they went to bed. They would fall asleep instantly when their heads touched the pillows. I gazed around the room, comforted by heated bodies moulded around me. The burning pain in my back kept me awake but I was loved and happy.

* * * *

It was fortunate I had an insurance policy before the accident. It provided me with enough money to fund the extra school activities. I had enough money to purchase a computer and started a small business as a pyrography artist. My office was on my bed, two tables which folded round my bedding. I did well and secured many commissions; portraits of pets, classic cars, and picturesque, quaint cottages were popular, as were house signs. Sporadically, I had people appear at my door requesting flower bouquets and buttonholes for weddings. Mostly it was by word of mouth, and customers provided the flowers and materials. My task was to use my creativity to give them what they wanted. At Christmas time, I received many orders, including making candle and table decorations. The money it brought paid our bills. This raised my self-esteem to be able to still provide for my family. Though, I do remember this was the poorest time in our lives. After household bills and children's needs were met we only had around £15 a week for food. Amazingly, we managed for nearly two years until I got a teaching job.

* * * *

The following year passed slowly. I felt degraded every morning, lunchtime, and evening when a caregiver would come and half carry, half drag me to the downstairs bathroom. Once there she would wash me the best she could; I didn't have a shower or bath downstairs. It felt like I was being processed and packed on a production line like an irrelevant toy which wasn't expected to last longer than one season. It was always rushed and clinical, as the lady had many other people to help before lunchtime. I felt dead throughout the process; she had a knack of maneuvering my legs and back into undignified positions while rushing the rough cloth over my skin. It was a hit and miss movement. I remember the term she used: 'sort me out.' It was easier not to fight; dignity had been blown out the window the day I hit the concrete floor. I never thought the caregiver was at fault; her time was limited, and she had many more unsavory jobs to do.

What I learned by being disabled for a time was the loneliness. No one wants to talk, your caregiver is counting the hours until they can leave. They are doing a job for payment and are not your friend, although they pity you. Some days I longed for a decent conversation. Mental starvation isn't often recognized, though it leads to depression.

THE LADY IN RED

A ladybird tiptoed and dared,

to casually cross my white linen bed,

before she opened her wings,

tilted, shivered, and fled.

She landed on my window sill

and scurried across the glass,

throughout the day, relentlessly,

her will was on the task.

I sat transfixed in my prison on wheels,

contemplating her plight,

while seductively ravaging an éclair,

then the cream slipped everywhere!

I visualized an epic display, but composed myself
with valor,

then returned my chair to the shimmering light,

where changing winds, blew me out of sync,

when reality enforced a breadth of view.

Her pace had started to dissipate;

I willed my body forth,

but my crippled legs denied me!

Leaving me distraught at the mere thought.

Darkness killed the daylight,

and the lady's engine died!

Leaving me exploding like a tempest,

before a fit and cried.

I felt dizzy, I felt confinement,

my body gravitated to the floor.

Like her, I didn't fight it.

Like her, I was no more.

It took around 18 months after leaving my hospital bed before I could finally stand up straight. My migraines, though, had become my worst enemy. I kept a food and drink diary for a year, highlighting trigger foods; they *habitually* attacked each month and lasted three days. The first day started with vomiting, my temperature dropped, and my hair and body would go sticky after sudden sweating. The pain would force me to crash on the floor, leaving me at the mercy of whoever was around. The second and third day would be just as painful, though my energy would miraculously return at the end of the third day when the migraine dissipated.

My children would leave me on the floor or bed after the vomiting had stopped and cover me with a coat or a bath towel until I slept. Nicole seemed to witness most of these attacks and became in tune with my body. When I was ill, she often lay her body next to mine to keep me warm. I think this was because she remembered the accident and when she crawled over my body. She knew after the sickness stopped my blood pressure dropped, and I would become pale and cold.

I have been thrown out of coffee houses and walked over in the streets. Once in Norwich, when I was laid near an entrance in a shopping plaza, people strode over my body rather than speak to me or call an ambulance. Another time, I collapsed at a doctor's surgery while waiting to be seen. Nicole was there again beside me; the reception staff ignored my 14-year-old daughter when she asked for help. Luckily a doctor from the Malvern Surgery walked into the reception area, scooped up my body, and took me to a side room. He pulled the curtain across and wet my head with a cloth before telling Nicole to stand in front of the bed I was on in case I fell out. The doctor rushed outside to get me some migraine spray and gave me a double dose. He was another superb doctor who helped me. He said it was a hormone deficiency that causes my migraines, triggered by the head injury.

* * * *

It was not until I used the computer that I realized how badly my cognitive abilities had been affected; my processing skills were non-existent, hence, trying to learn anything which required more than one instruction became a mammoth task. My first job away from home was a typist at a solicitor's office. Clients' letters had been dictated onto a recording machine, and all I had to do was listen and copy the words onto the screen in a Word document. It was heart-wrenching, realizing some of the words didn't register anything to me. I had no idea what letters were needed to finish the task. I felt inadequate and stripped of mental abilities. The next few days I started work earlier, hoping extra time to read and listen to the audio tapes would unlock my memory. A few days later my boss called me into his office. He wasn't amused and handed me a pile of 500 photocopies of A4 sheets which I had just done for him. He had asked me to run off 15 sheets, which was one document, and staple them together in page order, 1, 2, 3 etc. I didn't do it. I couldn't link the pages. At that time, I couldn't even count properly anymore. I had pages scattered all over the reception floor, trying to put them in order. I kept getting lost on task when my memory went blank. I should've told my boss I was recovering from a head injury, but I was ashamed and embarrassed and preferred to let him think I was useless at my job. At the end of the week I handed in my notice, and although my boss wanted to talk about it I couldn't. After that experience I didn't dare apply for another office job, fearing my brain had turned into a soggy mess. All confidence disappeared. Mercifully, two weeks later I was offered a job in an estate agent's office, and my main position was as a receptionist, chatting with people and making viewings and mortgage appointments. This was within my capabilities, although I struggled to understand and taking down phone messages. Luckily, two trainees were territorial about the phone, eager to please. The exciting part of the job was showing people through houses. I'm naturally interested in real estate, with its architectural differences, especially Victorian and Edwardian.

The injury snatched my confidence and new issues arose, such as panic attacks and hot sweats. These issues were worked through while I was recovering. I'm amazed and appreciative my children didn't develop any related patterns, which would've delayed or affected their cognitive development. Amazingly, now I have a futuristic kind of confidence. I feel nothing can hurt me, and if I were told the world would end tomorrow I would take it on the chin and wrap my last hours around my family.

Chapter Four

One day a four-legged miracle appeared at my door—or, more precisely, landed on my lap.

My spirit was positively ignited when some farming friends from the Yorkshire Dales, Mick and Marjorie Alderson, turned up with this six-week-old Welsh Collie pup.

I was a teenager when I was introduced to these good people. They were friends of friends and good traditional country folk who understood my way of thinking because they came from a similar mould. I would help on their farm and sit beside their elderly mum who enjoyed conversation. In her 90s, this lady was still producing decorative tapestries, although she eventually went blind. As a young woman, she had worked the farm with her children (one boy and five girls) after her husband passed away. I had immense respect for her.

One conversation we had was when I asked her how she managed to work the farm and keep the children under control. She laughed, and said she pegged them out onto the washing line! Her face was quite resolved, then she continued to say each child was harnessed around their waist with belly band attached to the line. Apparently, this was the norm in those days. The image I conjured up in my mind made me smile: scruffy urchins running back and forth along the washing line all day long in all weather.

Initially, I couldn't understand why the Aldersons would bring me a pup. I was incapable of looking after myself, so how was I supposed to cope with a demanding puppy? I still couldn't walk alone more than a few steps and had to cling onto the furniture and doors to avoid a fall.

They knew me too well and insisted they couldn't take the little hound back (knowing I would fall in love with her as soon as they left). After my substandard attempts at protesting, Marjorie thrust the pup onto my knees and muttered about shooting off to catch the traffic home which was going to be a tiresome drive.

I peered over my left shoulder; the pup was beaming up into my scowling face. Before I could string a sentence to discourage her, she slid her tongue across my face, then her body rolled off the bed. I heard a pleading cry and slouched my body to see where she had landed. Again, her eyes were drilling into mine, and she righted herself into an attentive sitting position while her black tail was dusting the floor in excitement. Her eyelashes stretched and flickered, exposing her gorgeous brown eyes. I named her Jess.

She loved me from day one; her heart danced into mine, though I had no idea how I was going to exercise her. When the children were home, it wasn't an issue; they would bounce their tiny bodies in front of me like rubber balls of white light before running into the garden with Jess at the center of attention.

While my children were at school, I couldn't see any possibility of taking Jess outside. However, after two days of Jess's whining, I couldn't take anymore. I had to make it happen and reach the back door; a litter tray was not acceptable in the house.

Jess was from a family of sheepdogs and needed a lot of exercise to fulfill her physical and emotional needs. Spring was in the air, my children had trotted off to school, and I told myself that day my kitchen floor would be puddle-free. She paced back-and-forth which told me I didn't have long. I crouched over to allow my body to drop from the bed and dragged myself on hands and knees until I reached the door. The unseasoned red dog lead was on a low table; I clipped it onto Jess's collar.

The two of us must have been having a telepathic moment because she mimicked my every move. Finally, after many breaths and whimpering from my impatient pup I managed to pull the back door handle down enough to open, allowing Jess to run outside and relieve herself on the grass.

That was the easy part. Trying to get her inside was another matter. She never wanted to step back indoors. Why would she? A battle of wills would begin.

I was at an obvious physical disadvantage, and lots of tugging and pulling took place. It was as intense as a work out at the gym. It took a lot of effort and concentration for my body to connect with my mind. My emotions were out of whack and my right side was stronger than my left, which caused me to move in a lopsided fashion, like a crab at the seaside.

From Mondays to Fridays I went through this ordeal three times a day for months. Jess would always play coy until we reached the back door, then all hell would break loose while she conjured every thought imaginable to override me. I would battle to pull my body into a sitting position of sorts while gripping the door frame with my hands while Jess frantically yanked me to get to the garden. My fingers would grip the lead for dear life while Jess dragged her body out into the sunshine where she belonged. It must have looked ridiculous to anyone walking by.

More days gathered with seasons blending together and the initial exasperating ordeal was over. My body began to feel alive! I felt the benefits of the fresh air hitting my face every time I opened the door. I yearned for the outside again; I was missing a fundamental part of my life. The pain around my spine had moved and was noticeably lighter after Jess tugged away at me. It was obvious my arms and back were forcibly being stretched, and it was helping me. I suppose it was a form of physio, instigated by Jess. There were other benefits, too. She kept my mind alert and in a positive place, during the early days of convalescing. Without a doubt, Jess was helping me to heal.

From the first, she was a character, with her personality of insight and devilment. The children adored her, and she became the leader of the pack.

A handful of years later I was walking to collect my daughters from the Girls' Brigade with Jess, as usual, tagging along. Suddenly, dark silhouettes were virtually in my face. Before I could think, I was pinned in the middle of three men.

My neck had goosebumps. I could hear someone struggling for breath behind me, and I smelled alcohol blended with stale cigarettes. I stared up at a lanky man who placed his grubby hand on my shoulder, weighing my body down like a sack of old potatoes. I clutched my drooping canvas bag with both hands to my chest while staring into the eyes of the grinning man in front of me. I couldn't describe any of the men; it was dark, and it all happened quickly. Thankfully, Jess had taken in the situation better than I. She had been in the shadows, walking to heel, but this day she took the lead. A growl followed by a leap at the man who had touched me. She intended to bite, but the men ran off in different directions. I pulled Jess into me; we had an overwhelmingly emotional moment and ended up cuddling right there on the ground before continuing to our destination. Her tail followed her high spirits. This was no big deal for Jess. She was my best friend.

The day came when I met a different side to Jess. A new member joined our household, and we welcomed her with wide arms. Her tiny half-grown feathers looked like they were stuck on with super glue, they were so messy. Jess, on the other hand, kept her distance, sulking with serious intent, overflowing with jealousy. On reflection, she must have been worried she was being replaced and wasn't allowing her position to be jeopardised.

This blackbird fledgeling was panicking when she was dropped into my happy hands one Sunday morning. A friend, Linda, had brought her to me after church. One of her cats had brought the bird into her house and was playing with it like a toy while the other two cats waited patiently to join in. Luckily, she got home in the nick of time. Linda was wiping away her tears with her cardigan sleeve, at a loss for what to do, until she remembered I used to work for veterinarians and would often come home with tiny abandoned or orphaned creatures. I took pleasure in homing these sweet animals. I would feed them milk through a syringe to save them, and most of the time it worked.

I peered into the bucket. Suddenly, it nearly dropped to the floor when Jess intercepted and took hold of the handle with her jaw. She was ready to eliminate the little scrap of feathers; I could see how distraught she was. But I didn't respond to Jess straight away. I had to take the creature upstairs to the spare room for her own safety. The room was perfect, with a big window facing the south side of the garden where you could hear other birds singing and fluttering between the small trees. I left her on the window sill before going back downstairs to get some newspaper and a box to place her in. I used a soap dish for water and had some bird food kept in a cupboard for wild birds. At the time I had a pair of blackbirds living in my back garden. My mind was already planning the day to reunite Fledge (I named her) with other blackbirds. After watching my new friend pecking at the seed on the windowsill, I walked back downstairs and sat on the floor beside Jess. She refused to look at me, obviously sulking; she had lain on the hearth mat and deliberately turned her body into a dead pose. I brushed my hand across her silky head, but she didn't turn her face to me. I continued to stroke her and talk affectionately, explaining how much the little bird needs our help.

Jess understood what I meant and half-raised her head to look intently at me then slipped it back into its hiding place. She looked pitiful, and I loved her more than ever and continued to stroke her. I had to make her realise she wasn't being replaced by a cheeky dicky bird. I went into the kitchen and had a cup of tea with Linda, who wasn't as upset now; she knew I had it under control. After Linda left the children came home from school, throwing bags and belongings everywhere in excitement. It was delightful chaos for roughly 20 minutes until the little people told me about their day. This was the norm, and Jess ate up their attention. Though when she looked at me, she sent me on a guilt trip with her "feel sorry for me" look, which made me laugh. I was aware that Jess was the best manipulator in our household, but I didn't mind in the slightest. After all, she was the one who got me back on my feet.

While my children were mingling and laughing I tip-toed upstairs, not wanting Jess to see me. But before I got to the door, Jess had slid around my legs and was sat waiting for me. I was a little taken aback because Jess knew she was not allowed upstairs, but I didn't send her down because I thought she should be included in the task of helping the fledgeling.

I lowered my body to Jess's level, stroked her, and spoke to her quietly, telling her to wait for me while I checked on the bird. Jess looked at me with full understanding, then I slid my body through the door closing it behind me.

The bird was fine, just perched on the windowsill looking out into the garden. She had made quite a mess with the food and water, and body waste was painted white everywhere, but that was a good sign as it meant she was settling in. After I cleaned up the mess and chatted a little at the scrappy fledgeling, I carefully opened the door just enough to slide my body out.

Jess was forcing her head through the bottom of the door to glare at her rival. I let her size up the bird for a few seconds while my hand was firmly on her collar before saying, 'Come on, girl, let's go.' Once she saw I was ignoring the bird she was happy to come with me.

For the next couple of weeks, I made sure Jess got more of me than Fledge. Every morning and evening Jess came upstairs with me, she would sit outside the room trying to hear what loving words I was saying to Fledge. One of my children told me Jess was so bitterly jealous her head would stroke the door when I was on the other side with the birdie.

But time does heal all pain, and she became fond and relaxed about the little house guest. After I came home from work, Jess was always waiting outside Fledge's door. She probably waited for hours, listening to Fledge fluttering around. I wonder if Fledge ever felt Jess was there. If she did, I'm sure she would have made the most of it. I would go straight upstairs, and Jess would be excited to see me but then turn to the door more excited to see her new friend. I would open the door and let Jess come in with me now, but I would always speak to her quietly to make sure I was at the forefront of her mind, not Fledge. She knew the routine and seemed to enjoy watching Fledge flying around the room.

Fledge didn't look scruffy anymore; she looked like a lively healthy blackbird with a personality to match. She had a knack of teasing Jess by flying over her head which would make Jess's head spin round in confusion. Then she would land on my shoulders and start to preen her feathers to deliberately tease Jess, who would poke her nose up close. At one point, I believed Jess was frightened to get too close to Fledge because she didn't want to harm the bird. Her eyes were always burring with excitement, and she was fighting her instincts to snap or take a bite at the birdie.

Fledge was a tease and knew she was the flavour of the month; I had to be on the ball at all times with the two of them. The first time Fledge flew and landed on my shoulder, Jess wasn't amused and pushed Fledge off with her nose in a gentle but calculated way. I was impressed! I laughed. I couldn't believe a dog and bird were fighting for my affection. I whispered loudly and bundled Jess's head into my hands then, when it felt right, I lifted Fledge up with two fingers and placed her onto my shoulder and turned directly to look at Jess straight in the eyes. She glared at me in confusion, and then looked even more confused when I slowly bent down and sat on the floor. Fledge was directly within reach of Jess. Our eyes didn't stray from each other's for moments when I just chatted to my pup with sincere affection. She found it hard to concentrate and control herself; I could feel she was struggling now she had the opportunity to eliminate the little bird who was threatening her position in the household. But she didn't jump on the bird because her obedience to me was unbreakable. A wonderful moment then took place when Fledge put an end to the silliness. She flew off my shoulder and landed on Jess's back which sent Jess into a humming top-spin, chasing her tail, trying to look at the bird who was as comfortable as sitting on a tree branch. The temptation for Jess must have been overwhelming, and I was exceedingly proud of her and continued to stroke her head and neck to help her relax. Jess slotted her wet nose under the bird; my hand was firmly on her collar this time, but I trusted her to sniff Fledge. Fledge didn't mind at all and had no concept of danger.

Strangely, I think Jess was impressed with Fledge. She seemed to change her opinion of the little thing and just accepted her to the fold. After that, when Fledge snubbed her, Jess instead dropped her head on my lap for a cuddle. I was overjoyed they had reached an agreement.

I rewarded Jess with a good two-hour walk. We played and fooled about; she brought me sticks and any old balls she could find in the woodland which was next to a playing field near our house.

I now took Fledge out on our walks, she would fly on my shoulder and Jess would walk as close to my body as possible without knocking me over. Even a rabbit or hare in a field wouldn't pull Jess away from us. I had noticed when any person or other dogs came near the bird, Jess would stop them from getting to close.

I took the bird out, hoping she would just fly away. I often lifted her on branches and still she wouldn't leave us. I started leaving the bedroom window open in the hope she could see the other blackbirds in the garden, but she stayed. My bird was full grown now, and I was getting worried she was with us for life, until one evening. I could hear a cluster of birds in the garden when my mobile phone rang. I took the call and had totally forgotten about Jess and Fledge until I heard Jess barking frantically and turned around to see Fledge fly through the window and land on one of the giant trees in the garden. I put my head out to watch as another bird flew onto the next branch. They perched for some time near each other but not connecting. I wanted to stay, but Jess kept barking. She obviously wanted me to bring Fledge back in. I thought about it and decided I must walk away. There was a chance the other birds would kill Fledge, but she had no life with Jess and me. For the next few days Jess went quiet and sat outside the bedroom door, wanting me to take her in, but I didn't. Each evening before I went to bed I did visit the room and noticed bird food had been taken; I had intentionally kept the window open for her. I left it at that and didn't want to know her fate.

The house was quiet for a few weeks. Jess wasn't herself, and I felt the loss, too. Then, one morning, when we came back from our morning walk, the sunlight caught my eyes, and something passed my face. A few minutes later Jess was barking at me. That was when I noticed Fledge on my shoulder, like the old days. I cried with relief and happiness and was just going to cup her in my hand and look into her tiny face when she flew away as fast as she came. I sat on the grass, quiet and forlorn. Had Fledge returned to tell me she was all right and not to worry anymore? Could this bird understand how much I loved her? I hung onto Jess's fur, curling through my fingers as she lay over my legs. We had lost an important member of the family.

I took Jess walking one day or, I ought to say, Jess was walking me, and I felt pure joy. My body had adapted to the training pace dictated by my beautiful four-legged friend. I never minded, I trusted her and knew if I were to fall over she would be there fussing around with protection. Our walks stretched through woodlands and fields, and at first I worried I would lose her, but I had to let her stretch her legs and have a good bounce about. She was like lightning. Often, I stood on a small green hill watching her zig-zagging across a field overflowing with long grasses and wild daisies. The sun and wind would fall on her, highlighting her delightful form and long, curly black coat dotted with pure white patches. Before I'd realise it, she would be in front of me, greeting me with her wet nose and bright brown eyes. This pleasure she generated would fire me up enough to withstand the pain that would follow once I was back home, positioned in my half-seated pose while my muscles were fighting each other.

Nearly everyone who met Jess fell in love with her and tuned into her intelligence. They seemed to notice her devotion to me. But twice I did feel sad for Jess when she was shouted at and attacked with a stick by a man who walked his two Labradors. The man never looked happy, and his dogs followed his frame of mind. He had them on a tight lead, and they didn't have the opportunity to run.

One morning, Jess was inquisitive and went up to his dogs. They stood eying each other and I thought it was nice, until the man used belligerent language which could be heard all around the field. Jess was startled and backed away, but then she came straight back and tried to play with his dogs. The man dropped the leash, and they were gone like the wind with Jess in the lead. Jess rounded them up and manoeuvred them between the goal posts on a football pitch before she crouched, willing the dogs to dare to pass her. They were trapped but didn't seem to mind. Jess thought she had been such a clever girl and was doing what she was bred to do. She came from a farm, and her mother's parents worked sheep. This was instinct to Jess.

I walked up to the man, who was calling me every despicable name he could think of, then he pulled up his thin sharp stick and slashed it brutally across Jess's face. I got hold of my dog and took her away. There was no point trying to reason with this person. Jess was sad, looking at me and wondering what had happened. I pet and reassured her; she was my lovely girl who could do nothing wrong in my eyes. I slid her lead back on to protect her until we got far enough away.

While walking back, we heard a cry, and both Jess and I turned in unison to witness the man lashing away at his two cowering dogs with his stick. Jess looked with pleading eyes for me to do something, but I knew I couldn't. I was aware if I interfered and appealed to the man's better judgement my words would fall on hard ground, resulting in his dogs receiving more abuse. Sadly, I let my fingers wander around Jess's head while saying, 'It's no good, girl.' We carried on walking in unison. Jess didn't want to run anymore after that. We called it a day and went straight back to the car, both feeling deflated.

Regarding my relationship with Jess, there's no doubt at all that she was the catalyst for me becoming the Lady Walker.

A four-legged friend,

brought misery to an end,

when my body was weak and falling asleep,

she motivated me with her own brand of cunning,

and hoisted my spirits until I was up and running.

She witnessed my first steps

when I trembled and fell,

and licked me with worry until I was well,

then winters nights turned to summer days,

and six legs were lurching,

and four eyes were searching,

radiant and a new.

CHAPTER FIVE

My determined head was set. I told myself now was the time to walk. It was embarrassing to be bottom-shuffling and crawling at my age. I knew it was only a matter of time before the children would feel resentment towards me. They were witnessing my struggles and weakness every day. My stepdad had told me a story when I was a child, about the wounded soldiers returned from the First World War. Many came home with broken bodies, their limbs missing and minds troubled because of the trauma they had witnessed, the death and torture. He said they were forced straight back outside to do physical activity, whether they had limbs or not. The remarkable outcome was the recovery rate was exceedingly high. Self-pity and dwelling on negatives were not allowed. Although my confidence had taken a bashing, I was ready to hit back like those brave soldiers. I needed to fight off the black coat of depression.

Joe was still unhappy at school. Georgia continued having nightmares and sleepwalking; her eyes were always stone black. She hardly spoke and needed speech therapy. (How ironic it was when later this little girl would end up singing in musicals and operas and earn a music scholarship at Wells Cathedral School, one of the best music schools in Europe.) I concluded my children's behaviours and problems were accredited to my weaknesses and I was the only person who could put things right. I wanted my children to grow up straight and healthy. It was important that I took control before my children grew up to suffer anxiety or depression. They needed to believe they had the power to do anything they wanted.

I had always been religious and turned towards my spiritual side and began meditating. I went back to yoga, which my Auntie Linda had taught me when I was young. It was helping; I was feeling more motivated about all our futures.

I started walking more upright, always ready to save myself if I went tumbling, which was frequently until I had built up muscle strength again. I would often land like a parcel on the floor and lie for a while before I would collect myself and try again.

The weeks became months, and I was walking around the bushes and trees in the garden. Jess pulled me along much of the time; we still were having the occasional tug of war. I laughed and played with her and the children joined in and took her off my hands when they came bouncing in from school. This gave me time to finish my commissions—usually a portrait of someone's pet. I was getting more income now because the ladies from the Women's Institutes appreciated my artwork and asked me to do regular talks and workshops. I had also acquired other jobs working from home, writing envelopes, and making things with my hands because I needed to be self-sufficient and the children needed to see their mummy working.

Time went quickly, and my walking progressed well; I felt stronger on my legs. Every spare minute of the day that I was not working, I would go out and roam the Malvern Hills with Jess. I had no choice—Jess would collect her lead, watch my every move, and always had an inkling as to when I needed to stop work.

I loved the Malvern Hills and relocated from Herefordshire to Malvern just to be near them; this was where I was fully brought back to life. My favourite walk during this time was in West Malvern behind the clock tower, a steep climb with the most spectacular view once you reach the top. We would walk here most evenings, up and down, until my body needed a bath from sweating.

After we exhausted the Malvern Hills, I ventured to the Black Mountains in Wales, exploring Abergavenny and Brecon Beacons National Park. We also walked 'The Cats Back' and the 'Sugar Loaf

Mountain' (Y Fall), as well as Skirrid (Ysgyryd) Fawr also known as Abergavenny's Holy Mountain.

While I was on flat land, I no longer had back pain. Uphill still caused some discomfort. I felt I had a ring of dead fat around my back and waist; that area on my body was always cold, as if the blood was avoiding it for some reason. But the more I walked, the stronger my body became until I had no pain anywhere anymore. Daily, I was drinking lots of water and stretching out the muscles that had been damaged. The children were growing up, and I was three-quarters mobile. I still had the night-time burning pain, and my back still locked without notice when trying to sit up, and my severe monthly migraines still took away three days of my life when I was laid up in bed.

Mick and Marjorie visited one Christmas, when my back seized up without warning. We were slowly walking around Worcester Cathedral. I had a cane then, but it was cold outside and my back spasmed. I was left in a crocked half-upright position with my head tipped to the ground. My friends struggled to get me to the car, and with help from passersby, I was lifted into their vehicle and taken home. I refused hospitals at this point, as they never helped, and I would relax better at home with my children. They understood my body and knew the cycle, how to bring my temperature down, ensuring I had enough drinks; they were perfect nurses coated in a special quality one doesn't find outside a family.

Within a week, my old friends sent me a plane ticket to go and visit a friend of theirs who lived in Toronto. He was a doctor; they said he would give me answers. Mick had lived in Toronto when he was younger and had medical treatment himself. I was overwhelmed and reluctant to take the expensive ticket, as they had already been a godsend to me. We agreed I could pay them back when I was able. Mick was a Northerner and didn't let obstacles get in his way. His reasoning made more sense than my pride, and after careful juggling to find the right person to look after the children I was put on a plane.

FRIEND

A friend is simply a gem in disguise,

You don't see them coming,

It's a terrific surprise.

Their timing is perfect,

Just before you fall,

They gather you up,

And rebuild your wall.

They won't let you pay them,

They do it for love,

Then fly away,

Like angels above.

The encounter in Toronto changed my whole life.

Peter Ng was a doctor who listened to me and actually heard every word I said. I had a thorough medical examination. He took nine x-rays and before reading the results he gave an opinion just by looking at me. He was minimalistic with words, quiet in voice, and accurate with the eye. I had never been so impressed by a person before. He was small, slender, and big in unwritten knowledge. He asked me to sit in different chairs, had me walk around the room, then watched me bending to touch my feet. When I tried to walk on a painted black line in his consultancy room, I failed badly. He pointed to things on his wall, asking me to look up while he watched how I turned my head. He read all my body movements and my body workings.

Eventually, after an in-depth talk about my history, he asked me to sit down. We relaxed in each other's company. He informed me which vertebrae were broken and damaged. His assertions were confirmed after we looked at my x-ray results that same day.

He also noted I was experiencing pain throughout my stomach and it was severely inflamed because I had a grumbling appendix. I laughed at this because I also believed I did and often visited my doctor who refused to acknowledge it was anything more than the pain caused by my back injury. Six months later, back home in England, I was rushed to hospital just before my appendix burst. The surgeon told me I was lucky as it was in a bad state and obviously had been causing me pain for years. I had been in three hospitals over a ten-year period with suspected rumbling appendix but was always told it was impossible because, if I were experiencing appendix problems, I would be screaming and crawling all over the floor with pain. But I hold everything in. History had taught me to cry quietly when in any pain because noise just takes more energy from the body and it upsets other people around you.

Within a few months, I was feeling better. I was put on special herbal vitamins and given what I thought was undoable exercises. I had four weeks of regular acupuncture and endured intensive full-body massage workouts that made me cry with pain. He advised me to lose half a stone and never sanctioned redundant fat; extra weight weakens the spine and puts enormous pressure on the heart. It was documented that I must do regular exercise and push my body to the extreme, little and often, with plenty of rest and fluids.

I had total faith and belief in this man and his tiny practice. I went home feeling lighter in mind and body, my lower back pain was less, and I knew it was because of the intensive massage workouts. I continued with some treatments for a few weeks but had to stop because I needed the little money we had for my family. I did, however, learn about the importance of eating the right foods and more frequently. I drank loads of water and ate better when I could afford, too.

* * * *

When I met Dr. Peter Ng, I was having neck pain, pain between my shoulders, migraine headaches, low back pain, fatigue, and insomnia after the head injury sustained in 1999. Dr. Ng specializes in many disciplines of holistic health care, including chiropractic, acupuncture, natural supplements, and custom-made orthotics. Below is a word-for-word report, written by Dr. Peter Ng at Kipling Chiropractic Centre, Rexdale, Ontario, Canada.

> *Doctor's findings: There was pain response and stiffness of the neck noted at extension, flexion, left rotation and right lateral flexion of the neck. There were joint blockages, muscle spasm and tenderness at the C1,2,5,6 and T5,6,7 levels.*
>
> *There was pain response and stiffness of the lumbar region noted at extension, flexion and lateral flexion of the lumbar spine. There*

was blockage muscles spasm and tenderness at L3, 4 and 5 levels.

X-rays of the spine were taken on October 4, 2007. The cervical spine showed a marked loss of the lordotic curve and degenerative disc disease at C5-6. The thoracic spine showed a minimal left lateral convexity and a mild compression of the T12 vertebral body with about 15% loss of height.

Diagnosis: Cervical, thoracic and lumbar strain—sprain injuries associated with concomitant joint blockages.

Prognosis: Every moderate to major traumatic episode has a mechanical wear and tear effect on the discal and posterior joint structures. The frequency and severity of future symptoms depend upon number of factors. I cannot exclude the possibility of relapse considering all aspects of the case including her quite prolonged convalescence. It is likely that her spine will be subject to postural and mechanical disadvantages. I expect that there's an 80% probability of recurrent middle back and neck pain giving her symptoms and signs.

At the present time, this patient should continue chiropractic management for her rehabilitation. The progressive change and response to treatment is probably the best barometer of evaluation in the future to determine the treatment frequency of this patient.

Treatment recommended: The combination treatment is the most effective and natural way to relieve the pain. Everyone's experience with pain is different so treatment programs should be unique also. This program includes meridian therapy, acupuncture, chiropractic, electromagnetic and exercise therapy along with nutritional needs.

My nervous system had taken a bashing with the impact of the fall. This system is considered the most important in the body, and that is why it is the first system to develop in the fetus. It controls almost every action from movement, heartbeat, and cell growth. The brain controls and transmits electrical signals and nerve impulses down the spinal cord to all regions of the body and without them normal function of the body would cease. My body was having a lot of communication difficulties because some of the tramlines had broken away. My doctor at the original hospital said to just view my brain like a train track that has a few connections missing caused by the head injury. He also said that my creative side of the brain would escalate and become more adventurous. We laughed when I told him I trained in fine art, spatial design, garden design, and many more areas in the arts-related field. I found later I cannot correlate paperwork well, putting in number orders, and similar mundane computer like connecting emails, and understanding the workings of mobile phones is stressful for me. I cannot remember numbers anymore, but my creative writing has accelerated. It is interesting how the body compensates and works around disabilities.

My body had joined in the fight at last! The untangled muscles were on the move. Joe and Nicole would regularly pull and stretch my body out. One would hold my ankles and virtually sit on top of me to stop my body moving while the other would take my hands. Together, they would pull in stages, short and furious because they were so small they realized they had to give it their all straight away to have any effect. It was working; the harder and more adept they became the more relief I got. The burning pain between my fractures would often literally disappear.

We would hear my vertebrae clicking when they were being decompressed, and it was wonderful for me. I couldn't afford regular health treatments after the general assessments, so had to find my own way. In fact, it was a healthy way, no poisonous drugs or chance of an operation going wrong. After our sessions, the little bodies, eager for a reward, would jump on me and we'd all start laughing. With all the pressure I was putting on my body, by teatime I had to rest. I was going to bed at the same time as my children.

I was still willing to try anything to relieve the pain, except medication which often clouded my thinking. Though my mind had taught itself to disengage and filter through the pain, I conditioned myself to believe that I would always have pains and viewed it as a strengthening process.

While I was in hospital, I met two other people with serious back injury due to car accidents. Doctors suggesting to us that iron rods be inserted to support the spine. The gentleman was excited at the possibility because his spine was crumbling away. The doctors could only suggest 50% success rate and emphasized the need to think carefully and discuss it with his family before deciding. The lady who had been in a different car accident dismissed the idea and took the medication for pain relief. I listened to different views and ideas and decided to monitor and read my own body and do what I thought right for me. I paid for hydrotherapy and did exercises in the pool. I had regularly gone for weeks before I bumped into the lady who took the medical option of pain relief.

She had a caregiver holding her up in the water; she also had armbands and a rubber ring around her waist. I watched her for a while and noticed she couldn't even raise her arms because her muscles had worn away. She lived most of her life in bed unless a care-person took her out in her wheelchair. Her body had become thin, and her eyes had lost their shine and looked at me from dark hollow sockets with an opaqueness. I thought that could be attributed to medication, but it also could be depression. I have seen myself, friends, and colleagues who have been living in high-stress households develop this look of despair when they can see no way out of a difficult situation. This was always my biggest fear.

We recognized each other, and I went over to speak to her. She said she couldn't live without a live-in caregiver now and relied on disability allowance to pay for her living needs. I asked her if she knew if the young man had had the operation on his back, which he was considering when I left hospital. She said he had the steel rods fitted to support his spine but said the operation had gone badly because some nerves were damaged and now he, like her, lived in a wheelchair reliant on other people and his family for support.

I walked out of there thankful I had been stubborn and listened to my instincts and remembered the wise words from my stepfather. Everything he taught me when we talked during long hours of logging and rabbiting with the dogs was coming back to me.

When I young, I tumbled into a mass of stinging nettles after I fell off a wall during a climb. My stepfather walked in and picked me up like a puppy and lifted me down into the long grass before he hunted some dock leaves which he spat on and rubbed all over my tiny legs and arms that had swollen up, decorating my white skin with red blotches. My tears stopped when I watched his concerned brown eyes, and his confidence and his words took away the pain. 'Nettie, nature has its own way of healing everything.'

* * * *

When I was walking enough to start driving again, I found it exceedingly nerve-wracking. Basically, my back would lock without warning into a variety of L-shaped positions after sitting upright in the car for a certain length of time. My muscles became tight and rigid as if a vise had turned me, which meant I wouldn't be able to drive for a while. Turning my head would impossible once my muscles decided I needed to rest. if I were turning at a junction, I would be a danger to myself and other drivers. The only way around this was to drive for less time and keep stopping to get out and do some stretches or just lie down in the back of the car or even at the side of the road. Usually, Nicole sat by my side waiting for my muscles to relax again, then she would help get me up. At least three times, we walked into a corn or potato field and just lay there together, looking up at the sun. I recovered much quicker if the sun was warming me. Looking back, I can see the dangerous positions I put my children in, but what choice did I have? I managed the small school runs twice a day and drove to the local shop and playground in early evenings with my children, although as soon as I rested my stinging back pain would increase in strength. Eventually, my back got stronger, and I could drive safely for about 20 minutes without a stop. Over time, with repetition, my back stopped flipping out altogether; no more spasms and muscles tensing up. My independence slowly came back, and I could drive without fear on the motorway for long distances.

From all this, I have listened and learned to read my body. I was patient and rested when forced, knowing that was the only way I would recover. After leaving hospital, I had lost all faith in doctors in the UK because they wouldn't listen to me and only suggested tranquilizers to make me sleep, which was ridiculous as I had a young family to take care of.

Fortunately, while I drove in this fashion, my children were always with me, helping and encouraging. Often, they would lay me in the car and stretch my back and massage up and down my spine which relaxed my muscles. The little ones automatically looked for lay-bys and places to stop, pointing out and calling when they spotted a safe place. They were in tune with my body as much as I was. We never worried about how long a trip would take getting us to our destination and just laughed knowing it took me ages to remember information.

The longest drives were always at weekends because my girls were in musical productions, and we had to travel on the motorway to get to rehearsals. My wonderful children never complained or ever got upset with each other or me. They were good throughout and loved to play together. I haven't wanted to talk these things over with my children and they have never referred to this time in our lives. We have healed, and I have been lucky. I was at a low point in my life and could easily have taken a different path. But I think my children saved me. I doubt I would have found the strength or inclination to live had it not been for them.

Music bonded my family together. I was fortunate to grow up with music all around me, and this passion rolled over to my children. At one time, we had an old piano that I rescued from a skip, which was remarkably still in tune. We also had recorders, penny whistles, guitars, a violin, a flute, cornets, and whatever my children could get hold of. All my children were exceedingly musical. Both Georgia and I would always be singing. Georgia loved her singing and won a full musical scholarship at Wells Cathedral School, considered one of the best in Europe. She studied opera, violin, and some piano. Those were just wonderful days.

LITTLE FEET

Little feet, little feet,
don't grow too fast,
enjoy your innocence,
it's not going to last,

Little feet, little feet,
let your mind flow,
run in the sunshine,
dance in the snow.

Little feet, little feet,
don't look ahead,
darkness is evident,
stay in your bed.

Little feet, little feet,
let your love flow,
giggle like the child you are,
and follow your star.

Fifteen years after my accident I had the urge to ride a bike again. I used to enjoy bike riding, especially when there was a gentle breeze to rearrange my hair. Cycling is an excellent aerobic exercise which triggers the release of endorphins and I felt the need to feel good and stay fit again. However, when I tried cycling, it was a disaster. I managed a bizarre figure eight movement basically because that was the only way my body would take me, and it was impossible to ride in a straight line. I couldn't stay on a footpath or cycle lane—I needed the whole width of the road where the cars were. I kept falling off because I couldn't retain my balance. Not long ago I tried again and bought an old-fashioned bike, cream with a wicker basket at the front, romantic and French looking; alas, I still couldn't keep my balance, and I fell off every time. After exasperating attempts and too many tears, I gave the pretty bike away.

Then many years flew by, and a miracle happened when I went to America in 2016; I was encouraged by my lovely friend Kate, a physiotherapist, to try again on her bike. I laughed and explained to her that I will just fall off, but she smiled and said, 'Try it.' This time the feeling was totally different and apart from being nervous, it came to me naturally. The country girl from North Yorkshire was back without a care in the world. How was this possible? Why could I ride a bike now when for years I couldn't? Maybe it was the exercises I did to improve my balance? Or maybe the answer can be simplified: I was with a wonderful person who believed in me and surrounded by green woods of yesteryear entwining in each other's arms to reach the sun.

I used to be a strong swimmer, but that has changed, too. Now my swimming technique leaves a lot to be desired, even though I spent a month retraining my body and mind to swim again. At first, I was afraid to let go of the rails. Now, I can swim again, but do not ask me to swim in a straight line—it will never happen. I have entertained many an audience by using three swimming lanes to complete my laps, and I was not popular with other swimmers for obvious reasons.

These differences in my abilities have influenced my sense of humor. Before my accident, I was often a serious person and found it difficult to relax and laugh. Now, laughing and letting go has been part of my therapy, which has brought about its own rewards.

* * * *

For two years, I got frustrated frequently. My body wasn't cracking on the way I wanted; I was slow to get going. It took over an hour of struggling to get a good momentum going. I literally sucked hard to get oxygen into my lungs. The other walkers didn't have this problem; consequently, in 2016, my body went on strike. My heartbeat became irregular, and I lacked the energy to get out of bed in the morning. My hair had been thinning, and I knew I wasn't right. Doctors dismissed these symptoms and wouldn't investigate.

I tried to get a grip, but my mind felt clouded and I didn't want to talk to people anymore, even my loved ones. Friends noticed I was out of character. I had lost my glossy smile.

My health deteriorated more, and I struggled to work and walk around my tiny cottage. I changed my doctor. My new doctor was from a different practice. She listened, took one long look at me, and said, 'Thyroid.'

She took full blood tests herself and was spot-on with her diagnosis: Underactive Thyroid. I was relieved. Stabbing pains in the night would frequently wake me up; I was sure my body was forewarning a heart attack, like my parents before me. Twice midnight ambulances came out to me, and the paramedics noted my blood pressure up and down like a tennis ball. Tests showed irregular heartbeat, although after a few hours at the hospitals I was discharged when my body went back to normal.

The intuitive doctor was absolutely amazed I could walk out of my house let alone climb to Everest Base Camp only eight months earlier. In her opinion, I'd had this medical condition for a few years.

Within three months, new blood tests revealed I was getting the right dose of Levothyroxine (the medication used to treat hypothyroidism) for my body's needs, and my energy level was back to normal. The pains related to my heart had stopped completely, and the bonus point? My high cholesterol level which I had for years had lowered. Who would have thought a little thyroid could cause so much trouble?

* * * *

My back had not locked since I had the treatment in Toronto. My children were encouraging me all the way with kind words, laughter, and total belief that Mum was on the road to full recovery. I was fortunate to have their support; they never complained or made demands on me, never judged, or called me out for the embarrassing moments I put them through. They accepted me in my warped condition, and we all pulled together, rode the storm, and flew out the other side into the sunshine.

Obviously, when I got the idea to climb a real, big mountain, how could I be afraid? What was the worst that could happen to me? I had already been told I would be in a wheelchair and live on disability benefits for the rest of my life. The idea that I had been written off at a young age, considered of no use to society, touched a nerve. Where were hope and faith? What brought on this mindset of negativities being the norm?

I trusted my instinct, my earthly intuition. I listened to nature give me the clues and the answers. I kept my mind open and allowed time to heal me and allowed people into my life to share my ups and downs. Maybe I was just lucky and had a stronger body than most. I cannot say why I recovered and can now walk pain-free.

Over time, and with the help of friends, my young chicks blossomed. All their individual issues were addressed, and they are now well-adjusted, intelligent young people doing what they want to do. When Nicole left home, I felt redundant; I had a teaching job and lived in a cute little house but felt like I was missing something. I no longer wanted to work set hours; I wanted to work full-on for a month then have time off for travel. I changed areas of work and designed plans to cater to my new needs.

I felt now I was a Lady Walker; it was cemented in my blood, and it was undoubtedly an addiction. I walked Ben Nevis, the highest mountain in Scotland, and raised some money for the Alzheimer's Society at the same time. I found Ben Nevis to be a significant climb, with an abundance of wide stepping stones along the path area. And the Scottish people were friendly and patriotic; as one of my grandmothers came from Sterling, I was introduced to the bounty of Scotland years ago. I returned to Scotland to climb some Munros in the Scottish Highlands. Months after that, I walked the famous Three Peaks and then topped it off by going back to one of my favourites, Mount Snowdon, situated in North Wales. It is a great training ground and was used many times by the British Army as well as the world-famous climber Sir Edmund Hilary when he was preparing his ascent of Mount Everest.

Some walkers are much more adapted to walking down mountains as opposed to walking up. I'm one of those. Before I came down Ben Nevis, my walking pace met with the average member and my body settled nicely in the middle of the group. But once at the summit rain and mist danced through me, my feet were covered in snow and ice, and I scurried down as quickly as possible. My body felt like an icebox. I had bought all the right clothing, wind- and waterproof, but it made no difference that day. I was under no illusion. The descent was steep, and it would take me a long time to reach the bottom, especially when the ruthless weather was starting to cut into my face.

The boulder stepping stones, which were naturally smooth, cleared the way for rain to fall over. In a clutching and bumping scene of bodies, people were sliding around as if they were on an ice rink. My head tipped over the mountainside, and I considered the risks and believed I'd make it if I were careful with my footing. After leaving the path, my feet and my inner core warmed up nicely from the adrenaline rush. I turned my head one last time to see the army of bodies still scrambling about in confusion and knew I had done the right thing.

In some places it was easy going, although most of the time it was tricky business. I clambered over rugged boulders with small waterfalls making it exceedingly dangerous while rain was pelting me. I was coated in mud, and chlorophyll plastered green marks on my trousers. All I could focus on was getting to the bottom, so to speed things up I allowed my body to roll down a little. Then I fell on my bottom and gravity took off with me. Countless rocks were hiding under the grass waiting to trip me, but I was thrilled. I was a girl again, running on the river bank with my hair teasing the wind when life's intentions for me were a secret.

Time took daylight away, and my body started to ache. Finally, my feet touched a gravel path at the bottom of the mountain. After sighing with relief, I glanced behind me and up the mountain; it was still dotted with bodies, shrunken by the distance, trying to get past one another. My walking boots were squelching while the rest of me was soaked from head to toe. With hands feeling frozen, I waddled duck-like through the door at Fort William Inn, situated at the base of Ben Nevis. My left shoulder worked to push my body through the wooden doors. Instantly I was greeted with an abundance of light and heat radiating from a wall-sized fireplace.

I looked about to find fellow walkers, to share a moment of joy, but all the faces I met were unrecognizable to me. Just two sleepy bar staff and half a dozen locals who sat around a few tables. I felt the room had too much space due to the high-beamed ceiling with its octopus-shaped chandelier staring down at me.

My body was grooving inside, and I wished for someone to share the milestone, when I noticed one of our guides walking towards me. I recognized him; he was an accomplished climber who had reached the summits six of the seven highest mountains in the world. We had exchanged a handful of words during my ascent. I was elated when he spoke in my own English accent. North Yorkshire, it turned out; he was brought up just a few miles away from my birthplace. He bought me a hot cup of coffee along with his and was smiling. He congratulated me and said I was the third person to get down the mountain. I was fit to burst with glee. He said he had been tailing me for the half hour when he saw me sliding down the grass on my rear. I'm sure I blushed with embarrassment but laughed, encouraged by his wide smile. He continued by saying the only reason he didn't stop me was that he realized I was competent at rolling down hillsides, and was impressed, especially when I crouched and maneuvered my body without losing my balance.

Feeling tickled pink this A-grade mountaineer, an ex-paratrooper, thought I was adept at walking down mountains gave me a confidence fix. Admittedly, coming down has always been easy for me, I haven't had problems with my ball and socket knee joints like a couple of walkers I know. Probably because I'm a shorty of 5'4". However, walking up is a different story.

I never underestimate a mountain's power when climbing; all of Earth's forces seem to whip through you for their own delight and can leave you fully recharged and feeling more alive than you ever have felt, or drained and waiting at death's door. I never assume anything when walking their unpredictable paths. It is fair to say your character will change throughout your walk, depending on how you have been emotionally moved. I have witnessed climbers become stronger when they accept they must "go with it", and others can't bottle their emotions in and become overly chatty, excitable, or tearful. Part of emotional outbursts surface because of extreme cold, tiredness, frustration, or simply being overwhelmed by the realization that nothing is as expected. I call it "a chocolate box of spiritual delights". The physically strong and most energetic walkers don't always fare well on the mountain; altitude sickness doesn't discriminate against age, ability, or gender. It selects you or leaves you.

I once asked a guide at the beginning of a climb who in our group he thought would get to the top first. Silly me suggested the fittest; a personal trainer who was in his early 30s. The guide laughed and said he 'would never dare assume' and said he had seen many a weak-looking walker lingering at the back come to life on the last day and speed ahead of everyone. I have since learned he was right, reminding me of Aesop's fable of the Tortoise and the Hare.

I became frustrated and wanted a bigger challenge, one that would make me feel animated and push my body to its limits. My mind drifted towards Africa; I researched Kilimanjaro in Tanzania and knew it was my next climb.

CHAPTER SIX

I asked advice from a friend, John, who has miles on me when it comes to walking. Regarding Mount Kilimanjaro, he suggested I train over a two-year period to ensure I was physically and mentally ready. I took his advice, and between work and family all my time, life, and energy went into my training programme. It took a lot of perseverance to get myself into the right frame of mind.

Over stages my body readjusted, fat disappeared, and muscles strengthened. I became accustomed to walking in all weather conditions. In the beginning, I dragged my uncooperative body like a snail dragging its shell, but as the walking became easier my spirits lifted. I began to welcome the rain as it frequently showered me and embraced the backlash of wind cutting across my face in stormy conditions. Sometimes the timing was right, and the dark clouds would sit above me just when the sun had drained my body of its substance. And because I was hot and sweaty the fresh rain falling on me relaxed and cooled my body.

For me, the more walking I did the more my body craved. I became totally engrossed in the process and thought of nothing else but my goal. Soon, the exasperating training turned into a doddle, and it felt like I was honing a younger body. My mind would fling open the creaking doors of the past, and I would be singing to myself like a little girl without a care in the world, wandering the green and golden fields belonging to silver-framed memories with my first dog Micky.

It was not unusual for the odd dog walker to laugh at me and throw a hand up in the air to show solidarity. Especially on occasions when I lost my footing and was swept down the sandy banks adjacent to the sea where I lived in Corton until I landed on my bottom padded with wet earth. My once-new posh boots were plastered in dirt of all colors depending on which elements were in the soil, and I can't count the times I replaced my colorful laces.

Part of my training involved point-to-point walking. I gathered my gear and walked up and down Mount Snowdon, renowned for its unpredictable weather conditions. Walkers must keep a cautious mind as they plough over the steep, rugged path towards the summit, as the mountain is smothered with rich, sharp textures of uncertainty.

Finally, I knew I was ready, and all those months of hard training would finally pay off. The patient Mount Kilimanjaro in Tanzania, Africa was going to feel my small footprints, and my heart was beating with confident anticipation. I was no longer a broken body with a fragile mind, waiting to join the conveyor belt of those dismissed by society. The truth was, I felt better than before the accident, and in many ways I was a wiser person, more tolerant and mindful of others. I had been enlightened to the uniqueness of people who were invisible to me before. Many able-bodied people tend to socialize with the same, especially the younger generation. I think it is partly because they are too busy trying to get their own lives on track and because they are frightened of anyone with a disability. This concept is antiquated; disabilities are not catching and don't cause a feeble mind. In fact, these lovely people of strength and quality have a big story to tell.

Fueling my body with the right nutrition was paramount. My eating habits had to change to fit in with my new body's needs. I just thought of myself as a machine, which needed to be well-oiled throughout the training period. I ate the right food and drank the most powerful element around: water. This was all I drank for six months, and I must admit I felt wonderful on it and friends commented my skin looked fresher (although that could have been attributed to the excessive exercise and fresh air which I was treated to daily).

I don't drink alcohol or smoke, but I did have one addiction: coffee. I would often be propping up a bar in a Costa House in Malvern or Lowestoft, drinking lattes made with full milk. I was hooked on this creamy substance, and when I stopped drinking it I experienced bad headaches until the caffeine was out of my system. These headaches had their own brand, nothing like my migraines, more fore-frontal with a pressing feeling on my head as if a big hand was pushing me down. But soon it disappeared, leaving me feeling fresh and alert again.

I have never been dehydrated on a trail because I would drink about half a pint of water every hour. I had to force myself at the beginning until it became an automatic process. This was the right amount for my needs, but everyone is different depending on how much water and salt is lost through sweating. Fitness and the body's genetic makeup will also dictate how much water each person needs. I have witnessed strong walkers falter and not finish their walk because they forgot to drink and eat enough while en route. I knew I wasn't a strong walker with my health issues niggling away at me, but I wasn't going to lose a climb because I forgot to drink.

To make sure I didn't lose too much sodium through my skin I nibbled on salted peanuts and took my own salt supply everywhere to add to food. During a climb, my body was constantly fueled with rapid sources of energy protecting my muscles. I was warned about muscle damage which causes fatigue and loss of performance. Bearing this in mind, high caloric food, both sweet and savory, was often hiding in my pockets to satisfy my body's cravings up the mountain.

I'm naturally anemic and try my best to ensure I have enough iron to meet my requirements. I carry plenty of chocolate and dried fruit and have learned from other walkers that tinned fish such as sardines are a reliable source of well-needed protein, omega fatty acids, and other important nutrients needed to maintain the body, and it comes in the tiniest, lightest tin which is perfect to carry. Weight and heavy bags slow down every walker, especially me with my weak back. At times, when I was walking Everest Base Camp, I found the weight crippling and some days I couldn't even reach inside my pack to pull out my Canon camera. But what I see and experience on a mountain stays with me for life. It is documented in my memory to recap when I'm bedridden and too old to see.

Before all my big walks I trained with a full backpack to ensure my body had adapted to the extra cargo. The last month before a climb I walked with my trekking poles until they were extensions of my body. I found the poles to be invaluable when I was climbing Kilimanjaro and Everest Base Camp.

Friends repeatedly commented about my walking boots—they appeared glued to me. I literally lived in them and avoided wearing skirts or dresses. Partly physiological, the boots stopped me from falling; they rooted my ankles and feet when other shoes couldn't.

Although I took advice from professionals and bought the right clothing and food, and trained as hard as I could, it didn't stop me getting brain fatigue. It was when I was near Base Camp, I felt dizzy and unsteady on my feet, and I couldn't concentrate as well as the other walkers in the group, but I was lucky to be allowed to continue.

Apart from training on Mount Snowdon, I had four other areas which worked for me. Because I was living between two counties, Suffolk and Worcestershire, I had prime locations.

1) A 15-story building in Lowestoft, Suffolk, where I would run up and down the concrete steps. I found this the most difficult and uncomfortable training area. My feet never enjoyed pushing up and down the cold, lifeless concrete of a building. Each floor there had 12 steps. Without a doubt, my leg muscles and lungs were pushed to full capacity.

2) The sandy cliffs at Corton: walking up cliffs, over sand and gravel, was a new experience for me and I found it difficult work, especially when wet sand weighed my already-heavy boots. The cliffs were

frequently used by fitness trainers who pushed their clients verbally and physically to the point of total exhaustion. Strong men and women would run up and down the cliffs on falling sand which was happy to take you along if you lost your balance. I didn't run up and down but pushed myself repeatedly until I had no breath left.

3) The sea edge at Lowestoft where high concrete sides act as a flood barrier in extreme weather. Here, I walked carefully, stretching my legs back and forth over the concrete wall which nearly came up to my chest. I needed to be sure that my feet, legs, and back muscles got a full workout. I knew I would have large boulders to climb over and this was an ideal way to practise my technique. Always with my loaded backpack to aid my balance.

And finally, 4) The Malvern Hills, Worcestershire, Herefordshire and touching on Gloucestershire with panoramic views over the Severn Valley and the Welsh mountains and more in between. I chose parts of the hills which I enjoyed the most and what I believed would be more befitting for my task ahead: British Camp and my favourite—the Clock Tower situated up West Malvern.

I frequently climbed up and down the historic Clock Tower over the reservoir of North Malvern Springs. It is positioned at the bottom of a steep hill, which is paved with rocks and stones. I was fortunate to have these training grounds which left me feeling fabulous after a workout.

Severe weather training is a must for Everest, which is terribly challenging due to the time scale; usually after a week of walking seven hours a day a body needs to rest and repair. However, it isn't feasible when walking to Everest Base Camp, unless of course, you are wealthy and pay a pilot to fly you onto the mountain. For me, I would have felt cheated if I had cut corners. Walking on Everest drained every part of me. Although, I never had a negative thought.

I trained every day for two hours, building up gradually over months. When I knew a walk was coming up, I increased the time to four hours every other day, giving me a day's rest in between to ensure my muscles were rested. Then, a few weeks before a walk, I would drop back down until I only walked an hour a day, just to keep my muscles supple.

In the evenings, I rested and drank nothing but water. My eating habits also changed. I thought about what minerals, vitamins, and proteins I needed to keep my body's immune system in peak condition. I naturally have low blood pressure and anemia. Some doctors accredited it to having white skin and the red hair. (My mum was just the same.)

Throughout my training, I had my backpack and carried liters of water. I would be carrying my water and camera equipment up the mountain and had to get used to the weight, so my body would adapt. I had 19 long days of walking uphill with a heavy backpack to carry in high altitude.

KILIMANJARO

I felt ready. I had trained long and hard, I had studied information about the mountain, the country, and its people. I registered with a tour guide group for serious walkers like me who wanted a taste of adventure.

I flew from Heathrow to Addis Ababa and waited sometime before I boarded the plane which would take me to Kilimanjaro. The line had been ongoing, people kept pushing and shoving, and I felt smothered. I started to panic, my body was heating up, I sensed a migraine attack. I carefully walked onto the plane, sweating profusely as I went straight to the toilets to be sick, before falling to the floor crouched in a fetal position. My temperature was rising, and I had no energy to open the door. The plane took off.

I must have dozed a while before shouting and banging came through the door. Eventually, I reached the handle. Two distressed air hostesses lifted me out; they verbally pecked away at me like a couple of chickens wanting answers about the cause of my sickness. I could hardly open my eyes, everything was a blur. I slept for the rest of the flight.

When we landed, the staff helped me down the steps. They had been through my holdall and found a letter from my doctor explaining my condition which ended the panic. Understandably, they had been concerned about the safety of other passengers and whether I had something contagious. One of the air hostesses told me if they knew I was ill before I boarded I would have been left. The migraine continued having its wicked way with me for the next couple of days; one was the first day of the climb. I kept the secret to myself, walked very sluggishly, and hoped no one noticed.

Kilimanjaro is gracefully referred to as "The Roof of Africa". Always snow-capped, this mountain is Africa's highest point, situated in Tanzania, and made up of three extinct volcanoes: Kibo, Mawenzi, and Shira. The highest peak, Uhuru, is 5,899 metres. People travel from all over the world to experience the unforgettable climb.

The small group I went with was organized from all walks of life: America, Australia, New Zealand, as well as the United Kingdom. We all had slightly different perceptions of what lay ahead, yet we bonded in our mutual excitement. I believe you wouldn't be able to climb this mountain if your heart was not open and giving, and with respect for the mountain, I felt it should be this way.

There are various routes to the top, but I took the Marangu because it was the easiest to manage. It is recognized as the most straightforward route up Kilimanjaro. Nevertheless, it is full of the magic created by man's imagination of The Quiet Giant. The Marangu Route is also known as "Coca Cola Route" because it is popular, cheaper, and believed to be easier. The Machame Route is known as the "Whiskey Route" because it is perceived as a much harder walk. This can be misleading because more walkers fail to get to the summit on the Coca-Cola Route. Partly because some people assume it is much easier than the other routes, but I was informed that isn't the case. It is a 35-kilometer uphill walk, followed immediately by a 35-kilometer, knee-breaking descent. Going down mountains is often more difficult and can cause many injuries.

After my flight, my lodging for the first night was at Marangu Hotel (1,300m) on a picturesque tropical 12-acre farm plot. On a cloudless day, you can see the snow-capped mountain in the distance. The next morning, I was introduced to our guides, porters, and fellow walkers during a full briefing while a kit inspection took place. It was enlightening, fun, but had a serious edge impressing that the right attitude was needed. Over time, this mountain had unfortunately claimed many lives; most were the locals who catered for our every need to get us to the top, carrying, cooking, and rushing ahead to ensure our resting place was ready for us.

The porters reminded me of ants, relentless in their pursuit to get up and down as quickly as possible. Their bodies were laden with equipment and luggage for our benefit, and the wind of guilt did sweep through my mind. All through the climb, our guides kept saying, 'poly, poly', which means, 'slowly, slowly'. We just kept laughing, but their advice was apt if we wanted to avoid getting altitude sickness.

I walked mostly with the guides because I wanted to learn from their knowledge of the mountain. A flower, Dendrosenecio johnstonii, which only grows on Kilimanjaro, was pointed out to me. It produces large leaf rosettes on the top and, when mature, it looks like giant candelabra. After flowering, one tree can have as many as 80 branches reaching out in all directions. An abundance of groundsels evolved specifically, their leaf rosettes close when needed to protect the young shoots from the frost. Kilimanjaro is ideal for any aspiring botanist to do research providing they are well equipped for the ever-changing climate.

While casually discussing plant life, we moved on to the topic of animals or, I should say, lack of them. The guide said there were many rare birds and lizards around, and on rare occasions a lone leopard had been sighted. I visualized the leopard's striking sinuous body standing high and proud, its opaque green eyes staring down at me. How magnificent! In 2005, a lot of excitement was had when a frog (Strongylopus kilimanjaro) was discovered living high up on the mountain in ice-cold streams. It is an endangered species, and with climate change its existence is under serious threat. There were plenty of other animals on this mountain, but the Machame Route would have been better if I wanted to see any. My guide then pointed out how extremely busy this route was with people going up and down daily. I stopped to look around and contemplated; the path was like an escalator, bodies ascending and descending. Because of this, the animals would go into hiding.

My knowledgeable guide welcomed my probing questions and proudly shared his wisdom. He pointed to a smaller flat-topped mountain where the local people go when they have problems relating to bad health, both mental and physical. I was told the mountain had special powers and I didn't doubt it for a minute. I liked this idea much.

We passed through five distinctive ecological zones while walking up Kilimanjaro: 1) Cultivated farmlands on the low levels where you can see land being worked over by farmers. 2) Rainforest, which is covered with more fast-growing varieties of plant life. 3) The heath, moorland which is rich with alpine vegetation. 4) The barren lunar desert area where the wind plays aggressively with your hair, the cold oozing through your clothes and pores which starts to interrupt your romantic climber's thinking. And, finally, 5) near the mountain summit which is icy and snowed over. On the mountain, animal and plant life change as quickly as turning over the seasonal pictures in a children's book. From the moss beneath your boots where giant ants carry cargoes of fallen leaves and rotting tree branches to the movements high above of birds flying through the treetops. On a steep gravel path, which was parallel to a little stream for most of the way, we stopped at Kisamboni, a picnic point. It was a most enjoyable introduction to the mountain's riches. We saw a variety of trees draping their branches above us. Birds could be heard but not seen, though we did encounter the black and white colobus monkey and were fortunate when some blue monkeys came mischievously bouncing from the treetops; it was better than any performing trapeze act and all for our benefit.

At our first camp, the lichen dangling from the trees seemed to have populated and moved closer to a triffid invasion. The first heathers were scattered randomly, and golden strands of sunlight replaced the semi-darkness in the forest. We arrived at the Mandara Hut (2,700m), but before we rested, we walked another 15 minutes to take advantage of the view overlooking the town of Moshi far below Maundi Crater.

On our second day, we came out of the forest and into the alpine meadows blanketed by the sun. I was wearing as little as dignity would allow apart from my floppy hat, which incidentally matched my green boots. I took time to explore what complemented the mountain, touching the different textures of the plants and noticing the vibrant colours. I was surprised that there was no sign of life apart from a few small birds. The warm glow of the sun permeated our bodies; we were doused with vitamin D, and everyone felt high. A wide variety of vegetation and changing landscape grew around us while we hiked over rocky ravines until we reached Horombo Hut (3,720m), our bed for the second night. This had been a long day, and the air was starting to get thinner. We didn't linger too long before crawling into our sleeping bags.

We were well insulated as we began our last full day up the mountain; our only noticeable body parts were eyes and lips. We trudged a rugged path spotted with a variety of different rocks and boulders arranged between vibrant red and blue lobelias enhanced by sparse varieties of groundsel. I found it astonishing how the mountain could be divided into different compartments with noticeable cut off points, yet slotted together majestically like a work of art.

When we entered the rocky and lunar zones, I copied the exact steps of the head guide; my mind was making mosaic pictures and designs with the intensity of deep concentration. We passed The Saddle, a barren plain of desert between Kilimanjaro's peaks with hardly any sign of life but for a few kinds of grass and the odd flower that we were too tired to notice. I have always loved walking, but Kilimanjaro was the ultimate climb. From the beginning, I felt the mountain flirting with me, and I was falling in love with its rugged characteristics. Every day and night, a new canvas appeared, and I was hungry to see more.

The day was getting colder, and I had to protect my eyes from floating sand while struggling to hold my hat in place. The wind was whipping, but I continued zigzagging my way up to the top. Finally, we reached Kibo Hut (4,740m) which was the last and, without a doubt, the coldest residence I have ever come across. I slept with all four layers of clothing on, including my gloves and balaclava, and was still cold, cocooned in my sleeping bag.

After being fed and given a few hours to rest, we set off in the dark to the summit via Gilman's Point to Uhura Peak.

We all had our headlights on and were freezing before we left the hut. The only noise was our stumbling footsteps and the crumbling of rock and sand when someone missed a foothold. I couldn't see a thing apart from a vague light in the distance, so like a drunken moth I ventured into the unknown.

I had no headache or sign of altitude sickness but was starting to feel the cold in my hands. After some time, I couldn't hold my walking sticks. My hands felt like they were on fire. I told the guide that I was struggling with the burning pain and it would be wise to go back as I believed I was going to faint. He offered to carry me, explaining I was only 90 meters from the summit. I smiled inside at his suggestion but couldn't allow that, though I'm sure the young man was strong enough.

I felt I had done my best, though disappointment was starting to gnaw at me with the realization I wasn't going to stand on the summit. I fought back tears.

We went down the long path until we returned to Kibo Hut where he made me a hot drink. I was told later that I should have had mittens, not gloves, because the fingers can keep each other warm. My feet and toes were snug because I had layered carrier bags between my socks before we started the summit.

* * * *

I intend to climb Kilimanjaro's Machame Route next time but will stay longer on the mountain to explore the brazen plant life and the shy creatures.

Mount Kilimanjaro was my first introduction to the wonders of Africa. I was bewitched, and the scenery rendered me speechless for hours while I soaked up the mountain's essence, which fed my heart and soul. I would recommend this climb, with the changing layers, to nature lovers. Commonly, you are assured uninterrupted views of magnificence.

I was lucky, my body worked its magic, and no one knew the pain my head was in at the lower elevation of Kilimanjaro. Ironically, for the rest of the walk, I felt great and never had signs of altitude sickness or headaches. After the climb, I floated on clouds rimmed with gold and by the time I was back at Kilimanjaro airport. I could have walked to the other end of the earth. Everyone seemed to be buzzing with me, though they were strangers. People from all walks of life chatted and helped in creating a magical environment while waiting for our next planes. Everyone wanted to learn my account of the climb. I didn't openly say I had been on the big mountain—it was my boots and clobber that gave it away, along with the golden shine on my face and arms from the mountain's kisses.

My body was still firing electric rays two months later. I had never felt this alive in my life. Friends said there was a change in me from head-to-toe. My light skin was now tanned, my nose was quite burnt, and my hair flushed out into a straw color, but it was all worth it.

* * * *

After a few months of catching up with work and my family, I got to grips with hardcore training. I knew the next climb was going to be more difficult. Training took everything out of me. I was happy with the way I felt. My only concerns were the cold nights and illusive migraine—both I couldn't prepare for. Six months later, I caught a flight to Nepal, Kathmandu and walked to Mount Everest Base Camp.

CHAPTER SEVEN

On 29th May 1953, Sir Edmund Hillary, along with Sherpa Tenzing Norgay, joined a British expedition led by John Hunt, and successfully climbed to the summit of Mount Everest. After his climb, Hillary was humbled by the whole experience and devoted most of his life bringing about changes benefiting the Sherpa families in Nepal. He founded the Himalayan Trust, and together they built hospitals and schools. Khumjung School in Solukhumbu, also known as the Hillary School, is one such legacy institution.

Hillary went on to climb ten other peaks in the Himalayan region, as well as reaching the South and North Poles. A statue of Hillary permanently gazing towards Aoraki/Mount Cook was erected because it was considered his favorite peak. The Nepalese government gave Hillary honorary citizenship for being successful on his ascent of Everest. He was the first foreign national to receive such an honor. When not on adventures, Hillary lived quietly with his family in Auckland City. He died in 2008 at the age of 88.

* * * *

EVEREST: BASE CAMP

Lukla Airport in Nepal is considered one of the most dangerous airports in the world. It is exasperatingly overworked, distributing cargos of people travelling to and from Kathmandu, which is the main access for hikers embarking on their Mount Everest treks. The pilots are extremely skilful, having to rely on eye judgment and gut instinct from the cockpit. The airport does not have a control tower or navigation system. The consequence of making one mistake is a 2,800-meter fall from the cliff edge. The deprived runway is 460 by 20 meters. Our pilot went in circles until she was sure the small plane was capable of taking off safely. The take-off procedure was literally dropping off the mountain into the valley below.

Tiny colorful toffees were distributed to ease our minds, but my vocal cords jumped a little when we took off. The plane reacted similarly in that it took a while before it stopped bouncing about. The doctor who sat opposite me gave a reassuring laugh and pointed to the wondrous views out the window. Without a doubt, it was an exhilarating voyage, and I would do it again, and did, on the way back. Another stomach-dropping experience which fired up my adrenaline just the same.

Day 1/19, I arrived at my hotel, Tibet International in Kathmandu, feeling quite sedate and fresh. I met my fellow walkers, surprisingly all from the UK. They were confident and friendly; we sealed together in a bubble of excitement. I felt overwhelmed. We met Binod Aryal, MD, an Indian doctor from the local hospital in Kathmandu, and a senior Sherpa Dawa (meaning born on a Monday) who would be escorting us up to Base Camp.

For the first week, I kept to myself while the mixture of personalities unfolded. We were a relatively large group. I was used to smaller groups or solo walking, this was going to be quite a different experience. The doctor took time to befriend me after recognising my introverted tendencies. I found him knowledgeable about the mountain and the country. He had been working on a five-year project on the effects of high altitude sickness and had written many articles on the subject. His enthusiasm for the mountain was evident as we got further into the climb.

After we gathered for orientation, Dr. Aryal checked our blood pressures. We enjoyed a meal and general briefing about our 19-day trek before I danced to my hotel room and landed in the center of a welcoming bed, latching my hands onto the crispy white cotton sheets. I slept like a new-born and woke like a teenager, excited for the day ahead.

Day 2/19 was spent sightseeing and bonding. We were introduced to the medieval town of Kathmandu. Then ventured into Pashupatinath and visited Nepal's largest Buddhist stupa (a dome-shaped mound or structure used as Buddhist shrines). It felt like I had been flown on a magic carpet to a place lost in time. My eyes were captivated by its golden splendor, and my mind rested in tranquil thought.

Day 3/19 the weather was good enough to fly over the mountains to the town of Lukla, high up in the Khumbu region of the Himalaya. There we meet our porters and our Sherpa guides who were patiently waiting for us with genuine smiles. Time was spent blending into the atmosphere while yaks were loaded up with our supplies. Then we started our trek, descending 450 meters towards the Dudh Kosi (kosi in Nepalese means "river"). We followed this river until we reached the village of Phakding where we stayed in our first tea house. The scenery on the way was quite different to anything I had ever seen before.

We passed Mani walls and large boulders engraved with Tibetan Buddhist prayer inscriptions. I would have liked to know what the words meant, but our guides didn't speak much English.

Day 4/19 we walked north up the Dudh Kosi Valley to Monjo, where the Sagarmatha Everest National Park starts. This is a UNESCO World Heritage (United Nations Educational, Scientific, and Cultural Organization) site, considered to have outstanding natural importance to the common heritage of humanity.

A steep walk brought us to the market town of Namche Bazaar (3,500m) where we stayed for two nights to acclimatise and do some shopping. This small town is situated on a crescent-shaped mountain, and because of the slopes, it provides spectacular views of the valley and mountains. A settlement with roughly 60 homes, it was originally a trading post for exchanging and bartering agricultural goods from the lowlands in exchange for butter and cheese made from yak milk, until Tenzing Norgay and Sir Edmund Hillary climbed Mount Everest in 1953. This was big news everywhere and made an opening for other climbers and trekkers. By the 1960s, Namche was recognized as the base starting point for trekkers and Sherpa. The town found a new income opportunity by offering touring guides.

According to government figures, Namche is the wealthiest district in Nepal. Wages are higher, and there are plenty of hotels, bakeries, cultural museums, and of course a seducing stupa and monastery.

We changed our money for local currency and stocked up on supplies as well as explored Namche's shops which had as many items hanging outside as inside, rather like an Aladdin's cave luring tourists towards the gregarious traders. Everywhere we went we purchased our own drinking water because they didn't have many taps, and water from streams and rivers is polluted. (This is in contrast to when I walked in the Alps around Europe where all water was free and dripping from the mountains into your thirsty mouth, clean and tasty.)

Day 5/19 we followed a trail along the Bhote Koshi to the remote village of Thami, which is the last outpost on the ancient trading route over the Nangpa La pass between Tibet and Nepal. Then we crossed the Bhote Koshi, on a suspended bridge draped with colorful prayer flags blowing in the wind and sending us good fortune. Knowing the meaning of the flags did help our minds to stay at ease, all the charm and gentleness made it a relaxing affair.

We continued uphill until we reached the remote village of Thami (4,000m) to visit the monastery. The name "Thami" refers to the indigenous tribe of people living east of Kathmandu. We circled back before turning up towards the enticing village of

Khumjung (3,970m) in northeast Nepal. There are 433 households in Khumjung, situated near Mount Khumbila. Sir Edmund Hillary and the Himalayan Trust established a school in 1961, which presently has 350 pupils from the Khumjung area. This was hard hiking but the people I saw never failed to reward me with their humble disposition and welcoming smiles. They appeared not to mind how much life force they had to give to secure a basic existence. This realization hit me every time I walked through a settlement and forced me to confront my own inadequacies.

This was hard hiking for me; we had been legging continually for days with disturbed sleep, and now every step upward was starting to kick back. When our vertical destination was reached, we had one last drop taking us into the valley where our tea house was waiting. Though cold, the people dished out genuine smiles and tea drinks. We also had a daily supply of hot lemon drinks made with powder (providing Vitamin C) as well as garlic and ginger drinks, ordered by the doctor as a deterrent again altitude sickness.

Salads and potato meals populated the tables; potatoes are locally grown and delicious. Rice and mild curry meals were frequent but usually reserved for the Sherpa. Surprisingly, their star pudding was tinned fruit and custard (very homely). All these foods can be purchased in the local village, as well as bottled water and a quick sugar fix, chocolate. Our doctor was impressive; he gave us antibacterial hand gel before every meal to prevent stomach upsets. Without a doubt, that man was tops, he looked after us like a shepherd tending his sheep.

Later, we trudged sluggishly downward and seemed to make it just in time before my body gave up. It was always a boost once we started descending into a valley, our minds told us the day's walking was nearly over. However, we were also aware of the next morning when we would have a precipitous climb.

We enjoyed what is considered one of the most eye-catching walks on Earth, around and inside the Tengboche Monastery (3,867m) located on a hill near the Dudh Kosi and the Imja Khola rivers, home to the Rimpoche (abbot) of Tengboche.

It is also known as Tamagotchi Monastery and Dawa Cooling Gompa in the Tengboche village in Khumjung. It is the biggest Tibetan Buddhist Monastery in the Khumbu region.

This monastery had acquired international publicity, praised by Sir Edward Hillary and Tenzing Norgay when they climbed the summit in 1953. It was built in 1916 by Lama Gull, a spiritual leader of the Sherpas, but destroyed by an earthquake. It was rebuilt in 1989, though sadly a fire brought the building down again and another structural and foundation makeover was necessary. Fortunately, it was formally consecrated in 1993. The Greater Himalaya Foundation in Washington, D.C. provided substantial funds towards this humungous project. Sherpa custom stipulates that an exceptionally spiritual man must oversee building a monastery. This prestigious job was given to the present Nawang Tenzing Jangpo, who is believed to be the incarnation of the founder Lama Gulu.

When walking through the regal gate, believed to be the gateway to Mount Everest, I feel its worth, amazingly powerful, creating a spiritual movement inside me. This build is stone which has been lavished in attention from its creators. My legs and mind hesitated in unison, allowing my eyes to take in the overall scenery. It was shockingly profound. Its situ, in the peak area of Everest, stands together with its brother and sister mountains.

The monastery paintings were full of intricacy. Potent stories from a time gone by came alive in front of my eyes; in fact, the whole atmosphere swam between the past and present.

The statue of Buddha painted in grippingly rich tones brought a sense of peace. I learned many times; a path would open its smoothness to me if I kept my eyes and heart wide open like the sea allowing love to flow in and out with the tide of enlightenment.

Glazing wishfully into Buddha's eyes, I felt soulful and unworthy. There was a wall with the lotus flower painted, representing rebirth. I witnessed symmetrical circular designs, known as mandalas, coloured in earthy shades which represented the infinity of the universe. I viewed much more art and crafted details on the walls and lipped into the structured architecture. Monks were helpful, allowing visitors more time to meditate and soak up the holiness. Our group walked in respectively while a celibate monk sat chanting. I studied him, his shaved brown head and golden leathered skin highlighted a hard, though dedicated life, but he had a peaceful spirit running through him and I wonder how it must feel. I bowed down like a coy cat and seated myself on a prayer mat and became invisible.

His thick red habit choked his strong, sinuous form. His chanting ended abruptly, and monastic silence flooded the room, it was hard to maintain my still disposition, and I had to leave the tension was too strong—I caught my breath outside, if I had been a smoker then I would have lit up. The monk's faith and total sacrifice highlighted I was inferior spiritually. He was a master who understood self-discipline; I'm a reckless child in comparison and have much to learn.

We hiked a bewitching forest to the village of Pangboche (3,985m), situated in Khumjung and the base camp for climbing the stunning peak of Ama Dablam.

Finally, we hiked up to the remote village of Dingboche (4,530m), Day 6 & 7/19 where we spend two nights. This village has its own helicopter with a landing pad for emergencies. It is also home to the world's highest billiard parlours, and there's an internet cafe with satellite technology enabling connection with the outside world.

Day 6 we climbed a scenic route to Nangkartshang Peak (5,083m) illuminating dashing views to the Khumbu regions. It could be said nature transported me to another dimension. Here in front of my eyes stretched some of the highest peaks in the world: Lhotse, Makalu, Cho Oyu, and of course the king of mountains, Sagarmatha (Mount Everest).

We continued pushing our bodies until we reached the glacial lake called Dughla (4,620m) situated in the Solukhumbu region. To the south, the famous Khumbu glacier stood out like a raw slice of noble white scratched with blue marble. Exceedingly impressive and sophisticated; naturally crafted into the mountain. I walked on its smooth surface and took many photos.

After lunch, we hiked on to Lobuje (4,940m), one of our last stops with overnight accommodation. This route to Base Camp is well recognized for being overly busy, especially in April when hundreds of Sherpas and porters from the region pass through; carrying supplies with yaks unthinkingly sacrificing their bodies to help westerners achieve a dream. My conscience was stabbed every time I saw a gently natured animal being loaded on both sides to serve us.

We walked the edge of Khumbu Glacier; initially, I was shy thinking it may move around, but it was solidified into the crust of the mountain. I felt safe though it was a dry day. Our path took us up to the village of Gorak Shep (5,164m), situated on a frozen lake covered with sand and grit; once, the original Everest Base Camp when mountaineers from Switzerland tried to climb the summit in 1952. Eventually, Base Camp was moved further up the mountain just before the Khumbu Ice Fall. This icefall is situated at the head of the Khumbu Glacier and the foot of the Western Cwm, with an altitude of (5,486m), on the Nepali slopes of Mount Everest. It isn't much higher than Base Camp but is an extremely dangerous passage with ice falling from the Khumbu glacier. I had watched documentaries about this crossing and spoke to climbers and have been left with no doubt the risk involved to pass this point. However, if I hadn't a family, I would have enjoyed the challenge. On a daily basic ice melt and moves causing climbers to fall to their death. The pull to reach the summit is extreme and un-comprehendible.

The safest time to pass is early morning before the sun cuts into the ice frozen overnight; there's less chance of movement and trekkers are more able to secure the ladders and ropes. The Sherpas walk slightly ahead and fix and prepare the route to give westerners a better chance to reach the top of Everest. Many Sherpas have lost their lives in this spot and will continue to do so as the ice is melting more with the climate change. Hikers do not appear to be put off—the addiction is too powerful.

Around Gorak Shep, many people including Sherpas start to feel the effects of altitude. Some walk to Gorak Shep and straight away descend to a lower elevation and wait a few days to avoid becoming ill.

After a rest and refreshment, we had the option to walk up the "black rock" Kala Pattar (5550–5580m)—experts haven't agreed on a height. Although everyone concurs, it displays the best views from its peak having a dramatic close-up of Everest and is a desirable spot for amateur and professional photographers; this was the final stop before Everest Base Camp.

With clear weather, we headed out on the final climb to Everest Base Camp, tucked under the sparkling Khumbu Icefall. I walked to Base Camp looking and feeling like a zombie. I didn't dare try any extra movements to speak or move my hands. I struggled with each step, which felt like I was lifting weights attached to my feet.

My body was no longer my own, my insides had shut down. My mind still under the influence of medication was struggling to relay any messages to the rest of me. I swayed in movement with the doctor right there beside me. He watched my every move and just continued to talk quietly, his voice kept me going. All I thought was, *a few more steps*. Inside, I didn't hear or see anything around me, until I reached Base Camp, alive with excited human noises. Unbelievably, part of my body was there, too. The good doctor understood my hunger to finish—only hours earlier I was at death's door.

Our happy band returned to Lobuje (4,940m), which lies near the foot of the Khumbu Glacier, and where oxygen supplies are waiting for people with breathing difficulties. After an extremely cold night plagued with coughing, we descended for three days until we were back at Lukla. I was motivated by the good feeling of my achievement. At this stage, I didn't comprehend how far I had walked and what I had put my body through. Everything was overwhelming, and quietness took hold of me for some days. We had to wait at Lukla for some time before our plane arrived, because of dangerous flying conditions. This was normal procedure; the mountains send mist and fog down as quickly as rain falling. I cannot praise the pilots enough for their intuition with the mountain and exactly when it is safe to fly. Finally, the conditions were right; immediately we boarded our little plane and went 40 minutes back to the capital city, Kathmandu. I was excited for my second flight on the plane and soaked in every view of the Himalaya knowing it would be the last time I'd have a chance to admire such earthly wonders.

Back at the hotel, I was elated to have a hot bath; my hair was a tangled mess stuck together with sand and grit. I couldn't brush it; alternatively, I tucked it permanently into my woollen hat. When it was freed for the first time, I looked in a mirror I didn't recognise myself. It was knotted up like a bird's nest, I had to sink it into the bath and washed it repeatedly before it returned to its pliable self.

I spent another day enjoying the fruits of Kathmandu before flying back to the UK. I mused as a tourist, deliberately bumping into the nooks and crannies of the old town; still bouncing on my cloud of fulfilment. I bought joyful knitted Sherpa hats, gloves, and leggings for my family. The many shops I visited were majestic, posing regal colors and arrays of fabrics: rich silk, thick wool, and delicate cotton. I could smell the threads and cotton being painfully woven and stitched together by the Sherpa women. The traders' faces danced with smiles of delight while seducing me into a sale, a striped woollen blanket caught my eye—it had taken president over a patchwork quilt waiting faithfully back home.

That evening, our group were seated to a celebration dinner, Dawa and our doctor was there with his young son who was dressed to kill in his tailored suit enhancing his gracious smile. I think he was 11 years old. We table folk all had a smashing time together devouring our Buffalo steak meals with all the trimmings. I had never tasted meat that tender and delicious; my eyes and lips were drooling with anticipation when the waiter brought my plate, providing me with my iron fix. The meat was compliments of a yak which had been organically farmed at the low levels of the mountain. There was no doubt about its authenticity, and I doubt I would get the opportunity to try it again.

After enjoying our meal and table-talk, the other members of our group went to explore the nightlife in Kathmandu. Luckily, Dawa offered to drop me off at the hotel on his way home with his daughter Dafutee, who was one of our Sherpas. I was in need of sleep and wrapped myself in clean linens again. In bed, my mind wandered over the whole exhilarating experience, and I felt blissfully complete.

Each day's heavy trekking left me mentally and physically drained. By evening, I rooted into the lodges and tasted Sherpa cooking homemade, healthy, and varied. Considering all nourishment, including water had to be brought up the mountain from the valleys below by yaks and mules, I appreciated and enjoyed every meal served with consideration. Meat was off the menu; it would take too many days to reach the lodging places sparsely dotted around the mountain.

Once, I spotted with interest a lonesome rooster, halfway up the mountain, comfortably strutting his stuff and ensuring no one fell asleep. He was well placed on top of this old hut; his red and gold feathers were strikingly on fire in the sunlight. I failed successfully when I fumbled in my backpack to find my camera—he had no time for a dithering female and disappeared. A Sherpa told me eggs were often found lying around. On those mornings, we had eggs for breakfast, I noticed the yolks were very pale in contrast to the brighter yoke I was used to seeing in England, but understood it depended upon what grits and plants the chickens could find.

Along with odd chickens roaming freely, lonesome dogs roamed the mountains. I never noticed more than one dog at a time and wondered how they could breathe in the high altitude. Their coats had adapted to the extreme weather conditions, and an old dog's coat was short, tight, and fluffy like an eight-week-old pup.

Most of the lodging houses didn't have fridges or freezers and limited hot water. Occasionally at night, a stove was lit, and everyone congregates in high spirits around the flame, just like bonfire night; admiring its gift of warmth. The stove was always situated in the middle of the building, the chimney funnelled through the roof, although I appreciated the heat I categorically struggled with the smell. Wood is rare and valuable up the mountain, because of this the stoves were often fueled with dried yak dung. My throat was always sore after I had flirted around the stove.

At times, the paths were exceedingly steep, I had no option but to pull or lift myself up with my walking sticks, some boulders and stones were up to my knees; I wouldn't have kept my balance without them. But once at the top, I was lavishly rewarded when my eyes revisited the slopes where the suns golden rays directed me down the landscape.

A young Sherpa walking with me because I had secured my position at the back of the group, often pointed out things I may have missed such as the Banner Clouds which can only be seen on Everest and the Matterhorn. They fascinated me; often floating in single file at a fast speed as if they were on a mission. I would have loved to study these unique cloud formations. However, being the lucky girl, I'm, I secured a couple of photos before they disappeared.

* * * *

Tiny plants latched onto the many textured rocks as the river flowed. We followed the current often; its speed was shockingly powerful. I opened my mind to roam and visualised being caught up in a monsoon when all land trembled at the thought of being washed away forever.

Like the story of the Loch Ness monster which resides in Scotland and Bigfoot in North America, the Himalayans have their own legendary creature known as the Yeti. Tibetans call it "the magic creature" and tales of its existence go as far back as the 4th century B.C.

In 1953, the great mountaineer himself, Edmund Hilary, along with his Sherpa friend Tenzing Norgay, found footprints that prompted an exhibition to fathom the mystery of the Yeti. But like many before them, they came to a dead end.

Information from the museum reports that in 1938 Captain d'Auvergue, the curator of the Victoria Memorial in Calcutta, India, was on his way to the Himalayas, and was taken seriously ill. It is believed he was nursed back to life by a Yeti.

Another tale was about a Sherpa girl called Lhakpa Domani who was looking after her yaks, south-west of Mount Everest and was taken and dragged off by a black and brown haired large ape-like creature. She said the creature became confused and frightened when she screamed allowing her to break free then the girl watched the creature who was upset attack and kill two yaks by grabbing hold of their horns and twisting their necks. Nepali police investigated and confirmed large footprints belonging to an unknown creature.

In 1951, a mountaineer and photographer Eric Shipman found footprints 13 inches wide and 18 inches long. He took photographs for scientists to examine. The animal prints trailed the length of a mile. It was concluded, no one could match the prints with any animal yet discovered, and it was left a mystery.

Many people believe the Yeti could be a Tibetan blue bear, rare in the west and only known by bones and few skins. Or maybe gibbon, a kind of ape. And another theory is it could be related to a red or brown bear, which can grow to seven feet three inches tall. It appears all sightings have been above 6,096 metres (20,000 feet). The Sherpa people know the Yeti as 'dzu the', a large shaggy animal that feeds on their cattle. The Nepalese government officially declared the Yeti a real Himalayan animal in 1961 and made it their national symbol.

The enchanting city of Kathmandu, capital of Nepal, has a population of around 975,453 and it elevates roughly 1,400 meters. It was named after Kathmandu Temple, which is situated in Kathmandu Durbar Square, one of the old places where signs remain dating back to the small kingdoms of 500 B.C. Historic water fountains, statues, idols, temples embellished with golds, reds, blues, and greens. Tiles, stone, and woodwork can be seen everywhere highlighting the talents of master craftsmen. There are three Durbar Squares all under the careful watch of UNESCO World Heritage Sites.

Kathmandu has been a great trading centrer for centuries, being perfectly situated between India and China. Merchants spill golden words to secure a sale. Traders came from all over the mountains, bringing with them unique art forms which they introduced to each other through cloths, wood works, gold crafting pottery, jewellery, and foods of vibrant colour and spice scents. Other traditional occupations were farming, metal casting, woodcarving, painting, weaving, and pottery, creating art and sculptures made of wood, stone, metal, and terracotta, which was homed in temples, shrines, stupas, and palaces. The art objects are also seen on street corners, lanes, private courtyards, and in open ground. Most art is in the form of icons, gods, and goddesses. Kathmandu is recognized to own some of the most incredible artifacts worldwide.

I would have liked to have visited the National Museum of Nepal, as well as the History Museum, and work my way through the convoy of art galleries, as art is an area in which I'm trained and passionate. Their art forms are a combination of two magnificent cultures and religions: Hinduism and Buddhism.

* * * *

Roughly 3,500 Sherpa families are living in seasonal settlements and villages along the main tourist routes. Here we got our accommodation with good local food and drinks. In the villages, we purchased our water bottles that cost from 20-30 rupees (approximately 25 pence) per liter at the lower elevation and became more expensive the higher we walked up the mountain. I have paid over 200 rupees for a one-liter bottle, and while a few people complain, most understand it is fair because Sherpa and their animals must carry all water and food supplies as well as other provisions up the mountain to keep the villagers and tourists alive. That is inexpensive; in America consumers pay $2-$3 a liter just at a corner market, which is £1.75 in England.

Sometimes tap water is available, sourced from natural springs, but it does need to be boiled before it is drinkable because it is loaded with bacteria. Every precaution must be taken to ensure safety while trekking up Everest.

Some of the shops in the villages at the lower end were overloaded. I literally had to dart my eyes up and down and left to right to ensure I didn't miss a little gem like a small bar of chocolate, which is a real delight up a mountain. What impressed me about these shops was the Sherpa creative weaving and knitting, the colours of the wools and fabrics were exceptionally rich, I bought Sherpa hats, gloves, and socks to take home and they were cheap considering the wool quality and the uniqueness of the needlework.

In some villages and tea houses where we slept, we had access to Wi-Fi, but it depended on the solar power caught that day. We had to pay for the usage if we wanted to charge our mobile phones and contact the outside world. I left technology behind so I could be in tune with the mountain and its people.

Sherpa isn't an Indian guide, as presumed by many Westerners, but the people who live in the Himalayan region, bordering Nepal and Tibet. They live mainly in the mountainous region of Solukhumbu, east of Nepal.

Sherpa is comprised of two words: Sher means "east" and Pa means "the people". Denoting "people from the east". Sherpa people migrated from East Tibet about 500 years ago, which is why Sherpa dialect is similar to the Tibetan language. According to the Nepal Ethnographic Museum, Sherpa language is related to other Tibeto-Burman languages spoken in Nepal, Myanmar, China, and elsewhere in Asia. This community has around 154,000 members comprised primarily of Buddhists who believe Mount Everest is the home of the enlightened deity.

Sherpa were primarily known as nomadic cattle herders and high-altitude farmers, weavers, and salt traders. Their Himalayan pink salt and potatoes are well known.

They lived a quiet life before Westerners became curious about climbing Mount Everest in the 1900s. But this did give the Sherpa opportunities to provide an income for their families, working as mountaineers and in the tourist industry. They are famous for their mountaineering skills, and during the three-month climbing season, a lead Sherpa guide can earn as much as $6,000, before tips. The average Nepalese monthly salary is just $48.

Biology professor Rasmus Nielsen, of the University of California, has studied Sherpa genealogy and has found that they produce fewer oxygen-carrying red blood cells at high altitudes. Nowhere else in the world has this been found. It is normal for the human body to produce more cells to provide oxygen at high altitudes. The Sherpa have adapted over centuries and have more blood cells running through their systems than any other. Everyone, especially the tiny children, always had a healthy red glow.

I took a photo of a Sherpa child sitting on a rock. His skin on his face was absolute with blood red cheeks and lips. I noticed all the people had the same healthy faces and remembered when I was a child roaming from field to field everyone commented on my facial glow.

* * * *

I feel I cannot go on without mentioning a Sherpa I was honored to meet, called Dawa Sherpa. We were introduced at the celebration dinner at the Kathmandu hotel after my trek. He was one of the organisers and has his own trekking business. His son and daughter, guides in their own right, were up the mountain with me. I bonded with his daughter, Dafutee, because she was my daughter's age and easy to talk to. Dawa is from a family of yak farmers from the Lukla area. As a boy, he grew up quickly and left school while he was still in primary education to be the sole breadwinner after his father died. This man experienced the hardships and frustrations of not having an education. However, many years later, he was given an opportunity to improve the lives of Sherpa children surrounding the Solu Kumba regions of Nepal.

While he was taking a group of trekkers to Everest Base Camp, they listened to his life story and were humbled and felt empowered to do something to help. These wonderful people brought together a plan, and by sharing a common vision, The Classrooms in the Clouds project was born in 2007. It is a registered charity, and most donations and contributions go towards building schools all around the Everest region of Nepal, including the remote villages of the Solu Khumbu.

Dawa informed me that to date they'd built 22 schools for Sherpa children—a phenomenal achievement!

The UNESCO Institute for Statistics reports that Nepal is the 12th most illiterate country, and is registered as the 17th poorest country, in the world. Education isn't compulsory, and governments don't provide adequate teachers, which puts communities under extreme pressure to improvise and find other ways to keep schools running. This is a mighty challenge when the Nepalese are under the poverty threshold, in a third-world country, and often live on £1.00 a day.

Another obstacle to education is that many children must work at primary school age; over a million Nepalese children provide income to keep their families alive. Some are domestic servants, porters, carpet weavers, or even doing hard physical work such as bricklaying. In the UK, we haven't had child labor since 1833.

Amazingly, with all the disadvantages facing the Sherpa people, the children's exam results are exceptional. The children want to learn; they stay focused, positive, and are fully motivated. With the help of further education funding, the Sherpa community will soon have the tools to become more proactive in their economic growth. They are a proud, hardworking, and respectable people and I'm delighted I had the opportunity to go to their alluring spiritual country.

At our celebration dinner, Dawa offered me a job to teach Sherpa children at one of their local schools, but at the time, I had other things to do in England. I did give it some thought and was grateful that I was considered suitable!

After the first week on the mountain, my body settled into a slower pace, primarily because I was exhausted. I soon realized that I wasn't firing on all cylinders and, because of this, a guide was appointed to walk with me.

His English was limited, but the Sherpa made a nice walking companion after he realized he couldn't turn this tortoise into a hare. For nearly a week, he tried to get me to walk faster, but it was pointless. I had found my body's pace, and it didn't match his. Once he understood that he slowed down.

He stayed at the back of the group with me to ensure I was safe and once it was justified. I was shocked to silence when I slipped down a steep path coming face-to-face with a pair of yaks. We could hear the comforting sound of their bells giving us warning to remind us to speedily move to the side, allowing the animals to pass. They were always over parcelled with supplies, yet they never looked concerned. When I slipped at this critically dangerous point, my head went forward with my body following behind. Thankfully, the reflexes of this young Sherpa were quick, and he snatched me up before I had time to panic. I would have landed on yak horns for sure if he hadn't been there. After that point, he kept a closer watch on me; to show my appreciation I bought him Coca-Cola® drinks, which he loved. I bought these from the scattered houses further up the mountains. Most homes sold drinks, chocolate, as well as their famous Sherpa hats and gloves. Because I provided the drink he often shared his chocolate, I wanted to take photos and enjoy the scenery. Initially, he was rather frustrated it could have reflected on his skill as a guide, but to me, him being there and helping me along showed what an excellent guide he was.

I didn't know anything about him, and he didn't appear to speak in group situations, though obviously, he did with his own people. All the

Sherpa families we met kept shaking his hand, and they all respected him.

I asked him the key to getting to the summit of Mount Everest, because I'd been told that he had climbed it himself a few times, with wealthy American clients. He said he'd been to the summit three times, but it was extremely expensive because climbers need to spend about four months living up the mountain to become acclimated.

Some climbers stay around Base Camp for weeks at a time, periodically dropping 200 metres below for a couple of days before going back to Base Camp. Once they can sleep comfortably at Base level, their lungs are ready to travel higher.

If I were younger, I wouldn't have hesitated. But I wouldn't do that to my loved ones, and I realize I'm not strong enough or rich enough to attempt it at this stage in life. Porters and guides are expensive and necessary to take enough oxygen to get to the top and back down to Base level. He said after reaching Base Camp there isn't much climbing, only walking to the next camps, but weather conditions are extremely unpredictable, and lack of oxygen stops people from reaching the summit. I know my body well, it doesn't tolerate cold, and of late, the English winters are starting to aggravate my bones, suggesting I may need to live in a warmer climate for my ending days.

The higher we climbed, the stronger the sun's rays chipped into my face. My lips were cracked and often bleeding over the three-week period. My face was red in comparison to the other climbers. This is because I'm naturally pale, white-skinned, being a redhead. When I got home, my friends said I had a "panda face" from where my glasses had protected my eyes.

At one time, we were literally walking on the highest glacier in the world, called the Khumbu glacier. This magnificent icefall has an elevation range of 3,300-8,848 meters. The paths seemed to keep going higher and higher, and I'm sure it cannot have been harder climbing a stairway to heaven if there was one. But I loved the challenge every minute of the day.

Mani mounds are often erected in memory of people who have died up the mountain. I walked around a memorial built in memory of the Sherpa who died near the Khumbu Icefall, a dangerous passage between Base Camp and the next camp up.

At times, we walked close to the edge, but the views here were stunning, and I had no fear of heights. I found rock stepping was not practicable;

the mountain had taken care to keep us on our toes and not get complacent while footprinting its mighty floors.

We went from sliding and slipping on grit and fine shiny stones until we progressed onto small rounded stones before our body and legs had to stretch fully to reach over the next surface. Occasionally, I would pass large boulders that I could slide down; at least, I found this the safest option. It was always in my mind to be careful before I stepped since a fall on the mountain meant "game over" and I wasn't ready to leave the pitch before I had my play.

I'd trained a lot in this regard and don't experience leg aches, but I do have to be careful of my left ankle, which sometimes plays up. I find my walking boots do successfully protect my feet and ankles.

At this point my Sherpa was learning to handle my camera, he was happy that we shared the experiences together and I paid him extra for all his time and patience he eventually acquired. We walked across many suspended bridges throughout the trail, all the way up to the mountain and back down again. This was my biggest fear, and I spoke twice about it with the trip organizers before I booked, even then I was still apprehensive. I read up on the rivers and considered walking down the banks to cross the water. Obviously, that wasn't possible, so I just went for it.

When I spied my first bridge, I stepped back in trepidation. Fortunately, Terry, who is army-trained, was sharp in noticing my fear and took control, quietly asking me to hold onto his shoulders. I closed my eyes and walked over the first few bridges; initially I was quite vocal and shaky, but with encouraging words from the terrific group of fellow walkers, I learned to conquer my fear.

By the time we were walking back down, I let go of Terry for brief periods. I was moving across a suspended man-made bridge! This fear had been with me since childhood, and many people have tried to help. However, the fundamental difference was that I wasn't forced, pushed, or shouted at.

I was walking across suspended bridges without holding on to anyone. I started opening my eyes towards the end of each bridge. This was such a big achievement for me, and I want to thank my walking companions for building up my confidence and looking after me.

After our evening meals, Dr. Aryal would check each walker's blood pressure, pulse rate, and heartbeat. This was nerve-racking for all of us although, we tried to appear normal and enjoy our meal we were nervous inside. One man had a panic attack while he was being checked, but the doctor realized and waited until he was relaxed before doing another reading.

I felt like we were taking part in a cruel experiment, like The Hunger Games, when someone had to leave. This anxiety affected our readings by raising blood pressure, but our good doctor knew if we were healthy enough to continue our climb. Once we were well into high altitude, our bodies adapted; we produced more blood, which provided extra oxygen enabling us to breathe easier.

The concept of failing a medical exam was unthinkable; we'd all trained for this once in a life time opportunity to reach Everest Base Camp. It would've been heart-wrenching for any of us if we couldn't proceed. Fortunately, we all passed our daily medicals.

Each morning we'd set off bright-eyed and high-tailed, but by the afternoon our tails had dropped, our eyes were focused in concentration, and we were stunned to silence.

We progressed from spring chickens to zombies daily hiking between six to eight or more miles every day mostly uphill, apart from when we settled for the night in scattered tea houses provided by the Sherpa.

All housing was situated in the sheltered valley areas, which took around an hour to get to. Our aching bodies forewarned the further down the mountains we stepped the steeper the climb the following day. This recognition would cause my confidence to nosedive, bending my body, while negativity stirred my thought. However, these feelings didn't live long. With the fruits of the valley interrupting and sweeping my mind clean to soak up nature's amazing tapestry, it was always the view that kept me going. On the last week of trekking, time appeared to have slowed down, personalities were getting tired and loved ones were being missed. The Wizard of Oz favorite quote comes to mind: "there's no place like home".

Then it happened. We all stood in front of Mount Everest Base Camp having our pictures taken. Everyone was captivated by the beautiful day and proud to have made the epic journey. I had a couple of photos taken then had to retreat behind a giant boulder to be sick. I lost all momentum and was lethargic for a couple of hours before our mountainside descent.

* * * *

Before I reached Base Camp (5,363m), I started my monthly period, followed by migraines. I took medication prescribed by my doctor in England—sumatriptan nasal spray. I hadn't considered any implications of taking medication at high altitude. And within 35 minutes of taking it, my body flopped, and everything in front of me seemed opaque. I was losing cognitive control, but fortunately, we were minutes away from the last acclimation stop before Base Camp. A village called Gorak Shep (5,164m), which is situated at the edge of a frozen lake bed covered in sand.

Luckily, Dr. Aryal got me into a bed and took my blood pressure; my pulse and heart rate were out of sync. The doctor used a pulse oximeter, to check if enough blood was going to my brain, because of the low oxygen level in the air. He said our bodies normally adapt quickly and start producing more blood supply. It should be < 75% at 4,800 meters. My oxygen saturation should have been at least 80%, but it was never higher than 75%. Dr. Aryal, along with the help of fellow walkers, massaged my body especially my legs and arms including my fingers and toes to get the blood moving. I don't remember if he gave me any injections or what else he pulled out of the hat to keep me alive. I do remember the oxygen mask was helping when I was gasping for my life and how painful it was to breathe.

I was aware I was not alone because I could see/feel ghostly faces floating in and out of the room. Some of the men were holding my hands and whispering caring words into my ears. I could feel them willing me on. Their unclear voices were swimming into each other, but their warm energies blanketed me like the sun on a summer's day. I felt their goodness.

It couldn't move any part of my body, and my mind went blank before I fell into a deep sleep feeling the coldest I had ever been in my life, even colder than when my hands were burning from cold near Kilimanjaro summit.

The next morning, I opened my eyes, and Dr. Aryal was sat on my bed beaming at me with relief. The day before the look he gave me told me I was on my last lap. His stare from his eyes penetrated my core. He'd been willing me life.

He said my body's readings had gone back to normal and asked me what I wanted to do. This doctor was conducting a study involved in research at high altitude. A mountaineer himself, he was preparing to climb the summit and was often seen walking up and down Mount Everest on his own. He was always on the lookout for ill patients who he helped when he could, often sending them off to the hospital.

Being just a few meters from Base Camp, I walked with the good doctor who understood completely why I couldn't stop. At a very slow pace, he guided me until I was in front of Base Camp with my fellow walkers who had been patiently waiting. Terry, standing behind me, propped me up while Dr. Aryal took two photos before escorting me to a boulder where I vomited.

Relatively quickly, my head cleared and the next day I could walk back down the mountain as if nothing had happened. I knew I had been in a dangerous place but had no idea how serious it was until days later when he told me the only reason I wasn't put into a helicopter was that he didn't think I would survive the short journey to the hospital.

I felt privileged to have spent time with this man, later we chatted in more detail about what happened up the mountain. We agreed that it was likely I had anemia and hypothyroidism before I started the EBC Trek. Anemia is one of the main causes of difficulty in breathing in the highland. But this could have been avoided, I did seek my own doctor's advice back home before I took up the challenge, it is on my medical records that I have an iron deficiency.

When I flew home to England a month later, I was still recovering from a severe chest infection. Over the Christmas period, I was admitted to hospital twice with borderline pneumonia. I was lucky; my lungs recovered and left no damage. I will continue walking up mountains, but I learned a valid lesson, next time I go into high altitude I'll spend more time consulting with my doctor regarding unforeseen events. If I'm told I'm not strong enough I won't walk. I have been blessed with immense pleasure already. I noticed while 4,000 meters above sea level, our doctor treated many walkers going up and down the mountain for free. He advised two Chinese men to get off the mountain quickly, one man was seriously ill with fluid around his lungs. Two other people were flown off in patrolling helicopters, which always hovered like red dragonflies flickering in the sun and moonlight. Experiencing all this impressed upon me the hidden dangers related to climbing mountains.

* * * *

Considering I've been hit with altitude sickness, I thought I would share what I have learned:

• Always discuss your health with your doctor before any climb, as studies show that people react differently.

• Ladies are encouraged to avoid going into high altitude when menstruating; blood loss means less oxygen to breath.

• Acetazolamide

• On reflection, it wouldn't have helped if I'd taken time-release Diamox tablets (Acetazolamide) which have helped other walkers avoid sickness and headaches at high altitude. I was told they work well with acetaminophen and/or ibuprofen. Your own doctor would likely help you with this.

• Throughout the last three years, mountaineers and walking guides I have met on track have suggested diverse types of marijuana. I looked in to this when I came home, and many local mountain walkers take cannabis which they believe helps prevent altitude sickness.

CHAPTER EIGHT

Geologically speaking, the Himalaya, including Mount Everest, is quite young. The mountains started to form over 65 million years ago, when the Eurasian plate and the Indo-Australian plate collided, which caused the Indian sub-continent to move and crash into Asia. These plates then folded into each other and pushed the plate boundaries into the Himalaya, it is believed the Indian plate moved forward about 1.7 inches a year and was gradually pushed under the Eurasian plate. The consequence forced the Himalayan range and the Tibetan plateau to rise from five to ten millimetres a year. Geologists believe that India will continue moving northward covering nearly a thousand miles over the next ten million years.

Everest is comprised of solidified sediments that once lay at the bottom of the Tethys Sea (an ocean that existed between the continents of Gondwana and Laurasia in the Mesozoic era before the opening of the Indian and Atlantic oceans during the Cretaceous period).

At the summit of Everest is the Qomolangma Formation, made of layers of Ordovician-age limestone, recrystallised dolomite, siltstone, and laminae. The formation starts at 8,600 meters at a fault zone above the North Col and ends on the summit.

The North Col is the sharp-edged pass that has been cut out by glaciers in the ridge that connects Mount Everest in Nepal and Changtse in Tibet, China. This connection makes the head of the East Rongbuk Glacier.

The North Col Formation is the next layer down, located between 7,000 and 8,600 meters, but is divided into several individual sections. The upper 400 metres is the Yellow Band, a yellowish-brown rock band of marble phyllite. Below the Yellow Band are more alternating layers of marble, schist, and phyllite.

Another 600 meters below, various schists have formed by metamorphism of limestone, sandstone, and mudstone, and at the bottom of the formation is the Lhotse detachment, a thrust fault that divides the North Col Formation from the underlying Rongbuk formation.

The Rongbuk formation is at the bottom of the mountain composed of basement rocks below Mount Everest. This metamorphic rock is made up of schist and finely banded gneiss. Between these rock beds are great sills of granite and pegmatite dikes where molten magma flowed into the cracks and solidified.

Avalanche, April 25, 2015

This earthquake was the result of the collision of the Indian Plate and Tibetan Plate. Nepal sits between the border of Tibet and India, which are still moving towards each other by two meters per century. The result is an earthquake of high magnitude registering 7 on the Richter scale at least once in a century. And if we observe the history of the earthquake in Nepal, a big one above 6 Richter has occurred once in 80 years.

Mount Everest is the Highest Peak and will remain the highest for the millennium. The amount of damage is influenced by the quality of soil and distance from the epicenter. If the soil constitutes soft sediments forming a loose grip, then the damage in the area can be higher compared to the other regions. The rocks on Everest are mostly garnet, granite, and limestone. The impacts of big earthquakes are felt on Everest, but the rock structure is hard enough to resist the pressure.

Every area of the community has felt the impact: the business industry, government service, education, local livelihoods have all faced the destruction of avalanche caused by earthquakes.

Many of the school buildings have been destroyed. Schools have remained closed beyond the academic calendar. Business, houses, and factories have collapsed, and many other government official buildings, too. People are living in tents and still afraid to move into their houses. But it will improve with media forces around the globe conspiring to improve conditions of Nepal. Japan, Indonesia, Thailand, Sri Lanka are Nepal's neighbouring countries who have experienced similar earthquakes. The Sherpa people acknowledge they can learn from this and put in place precautions to avoid it happening again.

NEW ECONOMY OF NEPAL

The short-term impact from the 2015 avalanches: Many tourists and climbers lost their lives that year, and the survivors flew home. Other countries put their nationals on alert not to travel to Nepal. Tourism declined and almost ninety percent of the flight bookings and hotel reservations for trips to Nepal in that year were cancelled. Many hotel owners and businesspersons also left the mountain and returned to cities. A lot of money and, more importantly, confidence, was lost.

But all things considered, Everest will remain to charm people around the world and tourists will flow into Nepal to see Everest and the majestic mountains. More people are being educated in Nepal than before, and many are becoming professionals in the Environment and Natural Resource Management areas will be experts in their field. There's a future here, money will be invested in the preservation of the mountains, and people will start investing more in tourism. More thought and money are needed to build stronger earthquake proof accommodations. All this will take a long time; Nepal is a poor country and needs time to reshape itself. But it will develop and continue to pull people from all around the world.

Everest Base Camp trail is open to walkers and was not seriously affected by the earthquake. The famous Lukla airport, which provides access to the mountain, was not affected, but the village did suffer some damage. The dazzling village of Namche Bazaar, where I stayed two nights to acclimatise, and most of the other villages I stayed in remained open for business. Some tea houses were seriously damaged, but it didn't affect the spirit of the people. And walkers will continue flocking to admire and purchase goods they cannot find anywhere else in the world.

There's always a conflict of opinions here; some mountaineers have said that they barely need crampons to climb to the higher camps these days because of snowmelt revealing bare rocks. Some Sherpa people are concerned and have moved off the mountain to live in the lower levels. If snow in the Himalaya melts, it is likely to cause a huge crisis for the people since Nepalese rely on the mountain water for hydropower, irrigation, and everyday living.

But this clear-looking water isn't safe to drink; it is full of invisible microorganisms that thrive in the millions. Bacteria such as Escherichia coli and Salmonella protozoa are found in human and animal faeces and will attack human hosts, bringing illness, causing disease, or even death, if not treated. All water must first be decontaminated to destroy waterborne pathogens. Even oral hygiene, such as rinsing your mouth or brushing your teeth, can cause illness.

Tenzing Norgay, who climbed with Edmund Hillary, believes the mountain is hitting back. Many officers at Sagarmatha National Park have pointed out that animals and trees are on the move and are going up to higher elevation levels than a few years ago. Monsoons are becoming more unpredictable, insects are flying higher, and there are considerable changes taking place.

The climbing world was shaken after the two avalanches killed 19 people on April 25, 2015. Thousands of people were left homeless, but recently and encouragingly, there's much support. Schools, hospitals, and homes are being rebuilt, communities are working together, and the wider world is becoming more aware of the Himalayan region.

THE BRIDGES

We had a lot of suspended bridges to zigzag across up the mountain. They were not suspension bridges, which is what I was led to believe; I was put straight by a Sherpa who explained the difference. A suspended bridge is the name given to a primitive support system. It has anchors at both ends, but no towers and piers like a fixed bridge. Suspended bridges follow a shallow downward catenary arc and can only carry people and animals on foot. Because of its limitations due to not having a flat surface, it is quite restricted to load carrying. But this bridge is invaluable and efficient with its sustainable design that is widely used in the underdeveloped countries. The Sherpa told me previously, the bridges were constructed out of wood and the whole community had to build the bridge by hand. When the monsoon visited yearly, bridges were often washed away, and those that did manage to hang on were rendered unsafe due to quickly rotting wood. When the new bridges were introduced to the mountain, they saved the Sherpa a lot of hard labour and valuable materials. Now, with the increase in bridge usage, the new suspended bridge is worth its weight in gold to its people.

I became quite flippant when crossing the bridges; I had stopped sheltering my body over fellow walkers and hanging onto their rucksacks. My balloon of confidence soon burst when I was abruptly put in my place. Heading down the mountain, I was on a rather long suspended bridge when I felt a strong presence and could hear heavy breathing over my shoulders. I couldn't turn around to look at his tall shadowed figure. I felt his weight when he latched on to me, causing me to drop down on the bridge with him over my back. He was trembling and bellowing at me to help him across the river. He said he was frightened of falling and couldn't move, which brought all my fear into the mix and I was temporally paralyzed. The other walkers had already gone and didn't know of my plight. I was alone with a heavy American man, double my stature, relying on me. I pulled myself up because the only way off that bridge was through my own steam, I couldn't close my eyes for protection or hold onto the sides because this man was gripping my body as if I was his only lifeline. I felt sick and was sure I was falling just as a light inside me powered me on. I commanded my body into the upward position and told the man to let go of me if he wanted to get across. I have no idea how we made it over the bridge, and he had no idea of my own fear and ran quickly without a word of gratitude when we touched land, leaving me transfixed while I composed my body and thoughts. A few minutes later, my heart sprinted with relief and satisfaction that I had helped someone who shared my fear of heights.

THE REGION

Because it is landlocked between India and China, Nepal is one of the poorest countries in the world, and its major industry is tourism, which only started around 1950. The people make eye-catching textiles including carpets, clothing, and leather goods. They also make and sell cement bricks and cigarettes. There are about 61 different ethnic groups and about 90 different dialects in Nepal. Sherpa, Tamang, Rai, Newar, Limbu, Tharu, Chetri, Brahmin, Kame are some. Sherpa is one ethnic group out of the 61, and the reason the world has heard more about the Sherpa community is because of the hard life they live, moving their homes around when Mount Everest orders them to.

These people are phenomenal; they never complain and never beg or ask or assume anything.

They're proud and respectful and want to rule their own country. They've been given a raw deal in their home situation; I feel any help the rest of the world could provide would be to the benefit of all humankind. After all, they home the greatest monumental mountain on the planet, and it is a world heritage, which needs protecting.

Nepal's landscape covers three climate zones running in a parallel east to west. The sub-tropical lowland of the Terai, which borders India, has the best agricultural growing conditions, and the main crop is rice. However, they also grow pulses, wheat, barley, jute, tobacco, opium, and indigo.

The next climate zone is in the hill regions. Here, more rice grows, along with maize and mustard (for its oils). Barley and wheat are harvested in the summer and vegetables in the wintertime; higher in the mountainous region, only potatoes can grow because there's less oxygen. But these potatoes are the best I have ever had and are recognised for their flavour and sold all around the world, along with animal feeds such as barley and buckwheat.

Yaks provide milk, meat, wool, and wondering chickens living between the first two ozone regions provide eggs. Although it appears many crops are cultivated and grown, there's still a shortage of food, and it is recently calculated that 50% of the area's children have chronic malnutrition. This is due to climate change and an increase in population.

New research by environmentalist predicts that the accelerating glacier melting up the mountains will cause even more flooding and less rain will be deposited into the rivers which will make life even more difficult for the people living in the Himalaya and beyond the borders. Another threat because of growing population is deforestation. Forests have been halved to accommodate the communities, and this has affected the quality of the topsoil which isn't as fertile and healthy as it was 50 years ago, now farmers are struggling to produce a good yield crop.

BLUE

Crepuscular means "twilight" in Latin; crepusculum appear when air density is lower at high altitudes, which causes air to bend, scattering light, result – bluer sky. I had 18 days of being surrounded by the angel colours (aquamarine, sapphire, topaz, and turquoise), which I was familiar with; I had studied the color wheel in art and delved into yoga and learned about the chakras. Many people believe these colors represent high positive energy to help motivate risk-takers who are seeking adventure. Could that be me?

I researched into the meaning of mani stones before I embarked up the mountain. However, they looked different to the way I had envisioned. They are formed from large solid rocks at the bottom, and over time they are carefully built up until smaller scaled stones are at the top which is higher from the ground. They are resilient and do not fall off; though it is probably a different story when the monsoon visits. A Sherpa does not plan when they create a mani stone; it must come from within when their mind is sitting in a good place.

Tibetan Buddhist Religious Customs

Throughout my time in Nepal and on Everest, I came across customs I thought were just juicily put together and wanted to delve into further. I put many questions to the Sherpa as well as read many accounts and formed an elementary description of my interpretations:

About mani stones, known as mani doh: A devout Tibetan will pick up a stone while chanting mantras before placing the stone on top of other stones, rocks already in situ. Eventually, a high proportion of these mounds will pile up into larger massifs. The Sherpa walk around these mounds in a clockwise direction to show respect to their gods.

Prayer stones are also common up the mountainside and in the cities of Nepal. In fact, I was informed they are positioned on sacred ground, but I do not know the rules about what is considered a sacred place. One prayer wall had an enormous amount of individual stones built onto each other; many were painted in eye-catching arrays of reds and golds.

An abundance of parcelled evidence declares that the dedicated Sherpa give their whole to portray respect to supernatural or natural deities.

THE SWAYAMBHUNATH TEMPLE

According to Buddhist scripture, called Swayambhu Purana, it is believed the entire valley was once filled with an enormous lake, and a lotus grew out of this lake. The valley then came to be known as Swayambhu, meaning 'self-created.' This name comes from an eternal self-existing flame over which the stupa was later built.

Many Westerners know Swayambhunath as the Monkey Temple because holy monkeys live in the northwest wing. They are holy because Manjushree, the bodhisattva of wisdom and learning was raising the hill that the Swayambhunath Temple stood on. It is told he was supposed to leave his hair short, but he didn't listen, and his hair grew and became covered with head lice. The lice supposedly transformed into monkeys.

The Bodhisattva Manjushree had a vision of the lotus at Swayambhu and decided to travel there to worship it. He recognised the valley would make a good settlement for pilgrims and to make it easier for people Manjushri cut out a gorge at Covary. The water drained out of the lake, leaving the valley in which Kathmandu now lies. The lotus was transformed into a hill, and the flower became the Swayambhunath Stupa. I love this concept and found Sherpa exceedingly passionate and proud of their unique heritage.

PRAYER FLAGS

Prayer flags are commonplace in Tibet, China, Persia, and India. The Tibetan word is Dar Cho, and "Dar" means to increase life and fortune, including health and an abundance of wealth.

These flags are put up in the morning when the sun has opened, and the people are happy and thankful to be alive. Nothing looks friendlier than streams of pretty, coloured cloth with inscriptions on them.

When the prayer flags are blown about by the wind, the ancient Buddhists believed the written inscriptions would bring about an outstanding spiritual movement, which would be distributed through the land and air. It is also believed, everyone touched by this event will be blessed with immense happiness. The Wind Horse, Lung-ta, is the most common inscription on the flags; this symbol represents good fortune and positive energies. The Lung-ta prayer flags are either square or rectangular cloths attached to a long string. These pray flags hang from a diagonal line running from high to low, attached to poles or high rocks. I noticed some were running from stupas, monasteries, and countless flags waved across mountain passes and bridges. Another kind of prayer flag called Darchor (Wylie: dar lcog means "flagstaff"), usually large, vertical, single rectangles attached to poles along their vertical edge. These large flags hang solo from tall stakes pushed deep into the ground to represent mountain, tree, rooftop, or a statue. Whenever sighting a flag, it is worth asking a Sherpa who will share a more justifiable reason for it being there.

The reason the ropes often run horizontally between two selected heights is that the higher the flag stands, the better the wind can work its magic. After reflection, I realize that Western society has adapted and picked up this wonderful tradition; we often have our own colored flags hung around our gardens and streets when we are having a celebration or party. We use them to make the occasion more attractive. We drape them over tables at weddings for good luck and fun. I didn't know the significance of height or colour until I visited Nepal. Now I understand more of their meaning I will use them to promote the feeling of harmony when the occasion presents itself, or maybe use them for decoration when enjoying the garden and watch the wind and sun do their magic and create a positive, spiritual atmosphere.

There are five colors, arranged from left to right in a specific order: blue, white, red, green, and yellow. These colors are connected to the five earthly elements related to Tibetan traditions. Blue symbolizes the sky and open spaces, white symbolizes the air and wind, red symbolizes fire, green symbolizes water, and yellow symbolizes earth. All these elements are needed to balance with nature, which is a vital part of promoting a healthy body.

Old Ways

While pulling my body up the mountain trails, I often noticed Sherpa women and teenagers carrying heavy baskets moulded into their backs; usually, firewood to feed their mountain homes.

It registered how hard life as a Sherpa living around the mountainside; I envisaged this vision would have been identical if witnessed ten years ago with the woven basket created the same traditional way. No matter, it was all in keeping with the mountain's requirements and the Sherpas were privately engaged in concentration on their footing placements; yet they graciously deposited a smile towards me and say "Namaste", meaning hello and wishes of good fortune.

The night times were horrendously cold when I visited in November and beginning of December, which was considered the end of the walking season.

After the trekking season was over, which was around the time our group was leaving the mountain, I noticed families were overloaded with their belongings. The women's and older children's bodies were carrying more than their own body weight, as were the yaks. Still, smiles greeted me as they left their mountain dwellings not knowing if they had a home to return to after the monsoon season had flushed its way down the mountain's heavy shoulders. I should imagine, well hoped that the families were going to catch up with friends and families who lived in the low lands, but I know they would have no time to idle but prepare to gather supplies to cart back up the following spring.

Bearing all this in mind I appreciate more than ever why food and water are expensive up the mountainside. No doubt, one of the first tasks is to rebuild and prepare lodgings before they can open for business.

Traditional Sherpa architecture shines everywhere not excluding the mountainsides monasteries. Their skill for marquetry woodworking is second-to-none. There's an abundance of trees growing on the lower level of the mountains, including pine and hemlock trees as well as a variety of rhododendrons.

THE BUDDHA AND SHIVA WALK

While trailing the river daily, it was alleviating to hear trickling waters in the background; sometimes it was gushing fast and furious as if its intent was being somewhere, another day, the waters were in a playful mood like little children having fun.

It was repeatedly said, 'The eyes of Buddha are always watching'. When I visited ancient monasteries, Indians believe Shiva's unclosing third eye is revealing the creation. The Hindu god Shiva has three eyes, the first two see life the way we do. It is considered we all view life differently depending upon our humanistic needs and has been called an illusion, whereby the third eye or brow chakra eye known as the "Eye of Shiva", is a symbol of knowledge that destroys evil and ignorance.

A friend of mine designs jewelery and uses the eye of Shiva in her work because many of her customers request it, a ring or on a chain, which they know is a symbol of good luck and keep evil away.

In Nepal, it is "Buddha's Seeing Eye" and is referred to as the "Eye of the World".

Temples in Nepal display the third eye of Buddha, which represents compassion and wisdom. All statues of Buddha paint a dot in the mid-brow symbolizing the third eye.

THE SAGARMATHA NATIONAL PARK

Sagarmatha National Park is in the Himalaya region with Mount Everest taking a regal position. It covers a vast area of 124,400 hectares in the Solu-Khumbu area of Nepal and animals such as musk deer, and pikas (similar to rabbits) reside here. I was charmed to see a pika, but he disappeared before I could snatch my camera. Our group was not fortunate enough to witness the Himalayan Tahrs, which are related to wild goats, and didn't get a glimpse, even in a dreamland of the elusive, stunning Snow Leopard.

The park is well cared for and has been recognised by UNESCO valuing its vulnerability, beauty, and contribution to the world. Geologically speaking, the mountains are relatively young and still developing. This phenomenal park with its dropping valleys and high dramatic mountains homes over 2,500 Sherpa families. It is believed there are 20 villages situated on the mountains. The Sherpa people themselves are conscious of the parks environmental needs and are proactive in the preservation to retain their culture. More Sherpa are being educated to understand the ecosystem, which will benefit the whole community. This amazing park is overloaded with flowers not easily produced with an artist's pallet. The rapid growing conifers provide abundant shelter to rare wildlife playing hide and seek with humankind.

ADVANTAGES AND DISADVANTAGES OF WALKING IN A GROUP

Within organized group settings, I'm slower than the average walker because my body dictates it. It needs a good warm up before it kicks into the right gear. But once I've pulled my body around the first hour, I can go on and on.

What I dislike is when the guide or a confident walker sets a fast pace. Generally, it isn't the average walker's pace, and other walkers become uncomfortable, but nobody wants to admit they are finding it hard. Many walkers have said this to me and that they didn't have the time to soak in the views or even time for a drink without a guide showing irritation.

In my experience, many guides and Sherpa want to get to the next stop as quickly as possible, everything they see on the mountain is old hat, and they may not realize tourist climbers want to walk slower. That said, the guards and Sherpa will have their orders and be given a specific time to reach a certain stop. I appreciate this to a certain degree and understand when we are being rushed because dangerous weather is coming.

I love it when a guide wants to share bits about the mountain. They know so much more than any book, it justifies the whole experience, and I'm happy to give extra money to an individual who has considered me. My mind needs to digest everything I see and feel.

Walking solo or with a personal guide is much more pleasant for me. Both are tied to the same walking pattern and automatically gel, looking out for the other. My time is my own, and I can take photos without rushing and feeling guilty because I'm holding up the group. And now that I have a slow metabolism (underactive thyroid) I will need more time to adjust so will leave group walking for the younger ones.

A mountain is a pillar of land gifted from the gods,

its power is too strong to compromise,

and its essence too extreme to dissect.

The earth's blood ruptures through her
commending rivers,

and wandering souls congregate in the valleys,

to feed on magic generating from the greenwoods

born centuries ago.

A mountain's unpredictable mood keeps the
walker humble and alert,

Sacrificing their body for enlightenment,

Madness or ecstasy traps them in her spiritual
flow,

offering sanctuary and an immortal glow.

Man cannot tame this radius of land;

it belongs to only life itself,

and if one tries to settle on her crust,

she will unleash her fiery tongue and send an
avalanche to sweep the intruder away.

CHAPTER NINE

When I came home, I sieved through my photos, recollecting precious memories, and was amazed there was no editing to do. I loved them all. With over 300 photos carpeting the floor I was back in Nepal. The photos illuminated the mountain's best attributes; views of rainbows and illusive asperatus clouds racing across the sky as if on a secret mission. I would never see this again. I was elated to have secured photos of Swayambhunath Temple before the earthquake damaged the magnificent build. Dolly mixtures of multi-sized rocks and stones, evolved over time, were randomly dotted underfoot, some larger ones seemed to have been purposely positioned by the Ultimate Being or a wise Sherpa. There was much to contemplate here.

I felt normal for a couple of nights after my flight, but I soon realized that I had not been freed that easily.

Over the Christmas period, I was taken to James Paget Hospital twice with breathing difficulties. I couldn't sleep lying down without blocking my airways. I was told that my body had taken a bashing and was close to pneumonia. Luckily for me, doctors said my lungs were not damaged. I continued to cough on and off for another month before I fully recovered. Throughout this convalescent period, I was sheltered emotionally and cared for by a great friend, Professor of Medicine Austin Yang. Some nights when I was struggling to breathe, he would instinctively call me to check how I was doing. His calm voice geared me away from panic attacks, he would stay on the line until my breathing was normal and I fell asleep. I thank him profusely.

Working and catching up with my family were the next priorities until everyone's needs were met and I felt I was able to have another wander. This time though, I wanted to treat my body, not abuse it. A few ideas popped into my head until I settled on the famous Alps Mont Blanc region. I was led to believe it would be a walk in the park.

Mont Blanc Horseshoe

After completing Kilimanjaro and Everest Base Camp in the same year, I rested and caught up with the mundane associated with life. I was wrestling with a chest infection even though my mind was roving elsewhere. My doctor suggested finding the sun to pull my body out of the slums of negativity. I'd finished a paid job and took his advice, thinking of a little stroll around those darling mountains in Europe, Mont Blanc to be specific. Fellow walkers suggested this would be fun and pointed out height and difficulty are not everything. Excitedly, I embarked on what I believed was a lighter walk, but I was in for a surprise.

British poet, Percy Bysshe Shelley (1792–1822) visited Chamonix in 1816 and was inspired. He wrote a poem in his romantic pattern called *Mont Blanc: Lines Written in the Vale of Chamouni*. Shelley plays with mythology yet acknowledges the infinite power of nature. This little gem situated in Europe, and inexpensive to get to, Mont Blanc was ideal. With warm arrays of weather in sparkling June, families casually walking up and down with no real gear to worry about or food to get steamed up for. I was fed on selected information portraying it was all modern conveniences and more like an artist's retreat than a climb.

I contacted an adventure company and was fired up, with two days to get my air tickets, paperwork, trustworthy green boots, walking poles, and floppy hat packed, and out of the door ready to face the encouraging sunshine. I explained to the tour company beforehand that I was apprehensive, as I couldn't speak French and had to make my own bus and train transfer journeys to get to and from destinations. But my mind rested when I was told, 'Ha! It's Europe everyone speaks English.'

Walking friends endorsed the simplicity of the adventure, and off I trotted. I caught a flight from Heathrow Airport to Geneva in Switzerland. My first destination was to the famous city of Chamonix, I knew it was a looker situated in the southeast of France. I booked into Mercure Hotel for one night. The taxi was an hour late collecting me, and other walkers, from the airport. I was hovering at the information desk, obeying my written instructions. I tried, with others, calling the tour company, but the number was dead. A lot of unguided words swam around the room for the considerable time before our driver materialized.

The French literally ran to us and abruptly checked our tickets. He sent one lady away in tears because her ticket was a photocopy—he was not in the best of moods. The driver gave us seconds to get our backpacks into the boot; he started his engine as we scurried to get into a seat. All the way to the hotel he drove like the clappers, cutting tight corners and shooting up the hills. We bumped along the narrow, uneven lanes, dropping off individual walkers at their lodgings distributed up the mountainside. All I heard was banging doors and sighing, and sometimes heavy breathing, all produced by our driver before he stationed his jeep outside my hotel. For some reason, I was selected for a bit of kind treatment in that the driver lifted my case and apologized for his moody behavior. Maybe my quiet-as-a-mouse demeanor appealed to him. Eventually, I was alone in my rustic room taking advantage of the oversized bath, before dropping downstairs to the barren restaurant. I gazed wistfully towards the mountain through the obliging windows.

The sleekly dressed waiter advised I delight in a special. After introducing me to fresh bread and olives, I was given a combination of barbecued meats with the best salad I had ever tasted. The waiter was Romanian and spoke English well. He tiptoed around me as if I was the queen because he wanted me to talk about my country. I didn't mind. After allowing my food to settle and enjoying the classical music at my candlelit table, I was yearning for the crispy layered bed. I crashed early and slept deeply.

In the morning, I met the rest of the team. We were a real dolly mixture, mostly women apart from two men. Five French, two Australian, one walker from Switzerland, two from Brussels, one from New Zealand, two quiet Chinese men, and finally a friendly young couple from Washington, U.S.

Once outside, we were climbing along the back wall of the valley until we reached Grand Col Ferret (2,537m) where we stopped for a considerable time. We pondered the waterfalls as they tumbled from crevassed glaciers. We could also see the long winding views to Courmayeur in Italy, a visionary experience for all. We then descended to the Swiss village of La Fouly for our overnight stay. After a seated feast of good looking food and wine, I homed into my bunk bed which was "well natures tipple" for me. The accommodation in the Alps was always warm, clean yet basic, but not without style.

Day three took us to the Swiss part of the Vale Ferret to Champex (1,450m) where we passed traditional Swiss villages and open meadows where local farmers tended their well-loved land. Our guide had quietly vanished and came back hours later, red-faced, which was fine—I had been active with my camera and felt energized. The views from this part of the trek spoiled us, they could have been from some ancient fantasy book; unfading colors with a metallic shine thanks to the sun. That night we bedded in a charming village called Champex.

On the fourth day, after being heavily sedated with richly buttered toast, we trailed down and away from Champex, and trekked around the Fenetre of Arepette (2,665m). This was a topping walk, holding the perfect climax to my Alps adventure. Throughout the walk, I was fed with golden humor from my new walking companions (three French doctors). Ironically, the women could speak no English, yet our telepathic moments gave us immense amusement.

We walked until we reached Col de la Forclaz (1,526m) where a vehicle was hanging around to transfer us back to Chamonix. An extravagant table was waiting for us, and the celebratory dinner was memorable; a lot of corks were popped, and our guides wasted no time getting senseless. The men rather liked this evening activity which they seemed to handle well. Every morning they were bouncing around like red balloons full of high emotional outbursts and positive spirit. Quite interesting, but I had an anti-social streak and tiptoed to my bed to dig out a book.

I found Mont Blanc to have one of the sweetest positions, complemented by its brother and sister mountains. We trekked on three countries in three days. 65km walking the Alps, up hill and down dale, chatting like vivacious birds, even singing at times. I was not weighed down with cold or wind but blessed with clear sunlight and nature's gold surrounding me. My camera never saw its case but worked for me; I glided through the printed evidence the next day on my flight home.

MOUNT SNOWDON

Mount Snowdon, or "Yr Wyddfa" in Welsh, is the highest mountain in Wales. Its elevation is 1,085 meters above sea level and like many mountains it sits in a national park: Snowdonia National Park (Parc Cenedlaethol Eryri) in Gwynedd.

On clear days, Snowdon puts on incredible displays of the British Isles, Scotland, Ireland, and the Isle of Man. A good camera is a must.

This is a grand walk I have completed many times when I was preparing for Kilimanjaro and Everest Base Camp. Its solid climb always left me wanting to return; mountains are proficient seducers.

Sir Edmund Hillary used Snowdon in training for his 1953 ascent of Mount Everest, and it is well documented that Alpine climbers generally acknowledged that some of the Swiss and Austrian Alps are tame in comparison with Snowdon. The reason being, most of the Alpine routes have been domesticated. Bolts have been drilled into the rock to make conditions safer for climbers. It has been argued that the decision-making has been taken away, dampening the challenge and adventure. Because Snowdon has not been tampered with, it has more raw elements of danger, making the challenge more meaningful to some hardcore climbers.

When I walked Snowdon the first time, I found everything to be on tap with a youth hostel in the valley below, and a hotel which provided quality meals. The locals were obliging and willing to share valued information regarding their beloved mountain in the picturesque area of Llanberis. My mind linked back to the film I have mentioned— going up a hill and coming down a mountain.

Snowdon is well layered with centuries-old myths. I was all ears when I heard of the legendary Afanc (water monster) and the Tylwyth Tag (fairies). The story teller's Welsh accent poetically spun the words, bringing the tale to life. A popular story flying around Snowdonia relates to King Arthur who supposedly killed a giant called Rita on Snowdon's slopes. The giant wanted King Arthur's beard in his collection. Understandably, Arthur didn't agree.

The name Snowdon is derived from the Saxon word meaning "Snow Hill"; snaw (snow) + dun (hill). While the Welsh name is Yr Wyddfa Fawr, which means "The Great Tomb" or "The Great Throne". All this folklore adds to the mystique of the mountain.

Snowdonia National Park is a natural reserve due to its rare spices which have adapted over time. The conservation programs are among the biggest in Britain, covering an 840-mile radius. Snowdon and its surrounding peaks are accurate examples of alpine environment: rushing rivers, waterfalls, valleys clothed in ancient woodlands with hills of green and gold. The mountain's valuable plant species are recognized worldwide. Many can only be found in Snowdonia, like the elusive Snowdon lily (Lloydia serotina), a delicate flower that dwells in compromising places of the Alps, North America, and of course, Snowdonia.

When walking around the Alps at the end of June, a tiny gem of flora was pointed out to me, with its numerous miniature flowers all delicately placed and giving their best side. The Snowdon lily is a flowering plant with thin, straw-like leaves that thrive in arctic-alpine regions. I haven't seen the flower on Snowdon yet; I need to visit when the delicate flower is awake and blooming. Once home I nosed the bookshelf and brought out my Royal Horticulture Encyclopaedias, and there she was. I was delighted I had viewed this flower personally.

Snowdon has bewitched adventurers, drawn many into its mystique. Handfuls have attached themselves, irrelevant of the consequences, to ensure they leave their mark. A prime example was in 2011 when walkers came across a Vauxhall 4x4 just 400 yards from the summit. It was a mystery how it got there, although, later a man was arrested and charged with a motoring offense. Another occasion to hit the headlines was when a man crawled all the way up the mountain on his hands and knees while rolling a Brussels sprout with his nose. This gentleman, who had the good sense to wear knee pads and a special nose protector, did get recognition and raised £5,000 for charity.

I often laugh about the last time I climbed Snowdon. One weekend, I was off to Wales when my daughter Nicole asked if she could join me. I was delighted. We drove to North Wales, but I hadn't checked the route on which the satellite navigation system was taking me.

I've had a fear of heights from childhood, due to a bad school experience. This fear was heightened after watching my mum freak out at a carnival. She tried to break out of her seat when she was stranded high on a Big Dipper ride that broke down in mid-air. I witnessed her hanging on to the thin rail while the operators were trying to get the Dipper working again. People had congregated and were watching eagerly from below. We could all hear the screams from the people stuck in the ride. My mum seemed to be screaming the loudest and was sliding out of her seat when the Big Dipper jolted and started moving again, to everyone's relief. My mum slipped out of her seat about 20 feet from the ground and luckily landed safely, though it was an experience to watch and her long wobbly body had a few bumps and knocks. But it was the look on her face that I remember: white as a ghost and of total disbelief. If I hadn't been so young and had more understanding, I'm sure I would have laughed like my stepfather and brothers. Instead, my look mirrored hers, and I held my tiny hand out to her which she snatched before shaking her head, and we both walked out mutely with our family following behind us still laughing.

From that moment on I'd been conditioned and couldn't walk up lighthouses and high bridges without screaming. Added to another trauma when I fell off a high wall into a nest of stinging nettles before the fall down the stairs which changed my whole life. It would to fair to say heights are not my friend. Yet, for some peculiar reason, I don't get frightened when I look down a mountain, I can stand on the edge of a bridge which is still attached to the soil. I concluded my fear was related to man-made constructions.

Nicole and I set off driving to Snowdon, singing on our journey, which was a normal style of traveling in my household. We were getting revved up by belting out the notes, excited about our adventure together when I noticed I was driving down steep mountains. I knew if I were walking the path I would feel ecstatic and alive, but because I was driving a car I felt I was going to lose control and drive over the cliff. I couldn't stop the vehicle because the path was too narrow, and it was the only way to get to the valley below where I had booked our youth hostel accommodation based at the bottom of Snowdon.

The steep road curved in a snake-like fashion with sharp corners. I panicked and screamed when I saw the sheer drop and realized I could quite easily skid off the cliff at any minute. Nicole had taken off her jacket and was holding it like a curtain across the window to limit my view of the cliff edge. At the same time, she was whispering to me encouragingly. My fears escalated when a car behind me started beeping, putting me under enormous pressure to drive faster. I blocked out the noise of that car and snail-drove until we eventually reached the bottom safely. I stopped the car sharply, before we both burst into laughter.

After we settled into our lodging, we walked nearly 300 yards to a hotel across a road and approached a group of local Welsh people happily talking in English. I asked them for help and explained my fear of heights, and what other routes I could take to avoid driving back up the mountains once we had finished our walks. The locals just looked at me then started speaking among themselves in their own language. I looked at Nicole, and we just smiled then ordered a meal and had a quiet evening together. The next two days we walked Snowden and Nicole was converted; she felt the power and wildness at the top and said she wished she could climb more.

We met many interesting walkers, some runners, and mountain bike riders whose faces beamed with enthusiasm as they zig-zagged down the mountainside. After another perfect day we went back to the hotel to eat home-cooked food and once more tried to make conversation with the locals. We were ignored again; we just laughed it off. But the third evening, when we went back to the hotel some locals greeted us like old friends, smiling and talking in English. Then an old boy pulled out full directions he had written, showing us a way to drive through some tunnels under the mountains, he said it would be an eye-glazing route around the seacoast. We were grateful, and enjoyed a lovely evening together talking about the local history related to the beautiful mountains in Wales.

CHAPTER TEN

My unconventional childhood, my shaky early adult years, and my accident helped to build me. I'm not broken, I'm reborn.

I hardly remember my mum. She was like a big black cloud that floated away by itself. My mind has been decluttered and reshaped.

I felt the child I was once, cushioned towards a bay window; life's unpleasantness and smiles rolled in and out during the day. I wanted badly to crack the glass and reach the other side—maybe I could stroke Micky again or run into my stepdad's arms and say the words he wanted to hear. 'I love you DAD.' But I never used that word.

I continue to walk.

THE FUTURE

After recognizing set plans never work for me, I will keep a wish list and see where I'm destined to travel. I will never lose sight of my walking boots. They're part of me. They dance me to imposing terminals to reboot my soul. I will remain unpredictable in movement, believing there are outstanding happenings for me.

As I write, I'm considering the prospects of owning my own semi-traditional narrow boat. I have been toying with the concept a few seasons now—it would provide a cute base to contemplate and grow. However, when autumn and winter knocks on the hobbit-sized door, I surmise I will have flown away with the geese to warmer climates.

The red dragonfly flicks her tail brazenly while securing a landing spot, energetically cutting the atmosphere of her domain. With amber wings merging into twilight She darts furiously.

Longing to salvage a life – but time is cruel to her; the success rate is low. She seeks a fallen body spotting the mountain's path and shimmers her wings before kicking off the unyielding rocks.

Her engine chokes passionately while racing in hell; speed is a must. Finally, she unloads her failing cargo in the mist of grey evening but doesn't have time to take a bow. Another walker is waning on Everest's crust. Extraordinary people who don't hesitate to sweep up her light. Nights run into days until her metal is cold and abandoned in retirement. Her broken leftovers along with lost lives feed the mountain.

Everest Walk, 2014

The colors blew me away, whites were whiter and blues just outstanding.

A homely feeling hit me when I noticed this little shop with
the name Kodak above the entrance, I smiled.

Healthy looking Sherpa child playing in rubble outside his home in Lukla.

This is one of my favorite photos, I remember trailing my weary body up the path, and glancing through the trees and there she was, 'the silent observer' watching and waiting for me. My mind stilled and my heart was reborn.

A great example of light and dark. The mountains atmospheric conditions ensured we had an ever-changing canvas.

A photo befitting for a water painting, with its soft array of colors floating into the atmosphere. I was surprised to see barbed wire which we have back home being used so high up the mountain, yet it highlighted, within beauty, there is a touch of danger.

My encounter with a Yak. As you can see there are many highlights on the path of enlightenment.

Paths beautifully designed by mother nature, to allow gushing waters to flood the land during monsoon season.

The higher I climbed, the stronger the suns rays caught my face. My lips cracked often, and bleed at the latter end of the trek. My face turned from white to red. When I arrived home I had a panda face, where my shades had protected me from the sun

Mani mounds erected in memory of people who have died up the mountain, either caught in avalanche or health issues relating to altitude.

Peaks. Scenes like this every minute of the day - how could one not be inspired to write this book!

Mount Everest, known in Napali as Sagarmatha, and in Tibetan as Chomolungma.

Me in front of Base Camp, Everest.

ACKNOWLEDGEMENTS

Writing my story has been difficult, but it has helped me understand the past and how I was as a young girl growing up in a dysfunctional household. It also highlights that good can come from horrific experiences.

Woman's best friend – Jess, I love you.

I appreciate a dear friend, Austin Yang, for being there when I needed someone most.

Dr. Steel, who gave me time and looked after me in hospital. I'd like to thank Dr. Peter Ng, who listened to me and heard.

Cally, you were inspirational and essential to my recovery.

I will be grateful to Wendy and Bobby for the rest of my life.

A special thank you to my editor, Michelle, of Modified Editing, who took some finding. I wanted to be sure I had an exceptional editor who would listen and feel the story. It wouldn't have happened without Michelle.

And a round of applause for my readers, for walking along my steps through time, and being witness to what some would describe as a miracle.

A Pebble

The sea whispered and waved to me

Begging me to tread the soft ocean sand

White frothing waters waded over my boots

Before returning to another land

I dipped my head to the ground

Where a sparkling pebble deposited from the sea

Brown and gold and smooth

Lay smiling at me with a fundamental beauty

I cradled the pebble in the palm of my hand

Then a warm breeze flew through my hair

I quickly pocketed my gift from the sea,

Knowing this is one find I cannot share.

In addition to her hiking and mountaineering, Annette is a multimedia artist (specializing in pyrography, photography and floristry), a reluctant public speaker, member of the Women's Institute and several Craft Guilds. She currently lives in Malvern-Hills, Worcester with her dog, Cheko.

Lady Walker

26344931R00153

Printed in Poland
by Amazon Fulfillment
Poland Sp. z o.o., Wrocław